Of Philosophers and

A disclosure of Martin He
Medard Boss, and Sigmui

CW01021788

Contemporary Psychoanalytic Studies
12

Editor
Jon Mills

Associate Editors
Gerald J. Gargiulo
Keith Haartman
Ronald J. Naso

Editorial Advisory Board

Howard Bacal
Alan Bass
John Beebe
Martin Bergmann
Christopher Bollas
Mark Bracher
Marcia Cavell
Nancy J. Chodorow
Walter A. Davis
Peter Dews
Muriel Dimen
Michael Eigen
Irene Fast
Bruce Fink
Peter Fonagy
Leo Goldberger
James Grotstein
R. D. Hinshelwood
Otto F. Kernberg

Robert Langs
Joseph Lichtenberg
Nancy McWilliams
Jean Baker Miller
Thomas Ogden
Owen Renik
Joseph Reppen
William J. Richardson
Peter L. Rudnytsky
Martin A. Schulman
David Livingstone Smith
Donnel Stern
Frank Summers
M. Guy Thompson
Wilfried Ver Eecke
Robert S. Wallerstein
Brent Willock
Robert Maxwell Young

Contemporary Psychoanalytic Studies (*CPS*) is an international scholarly book series devoted to all aspects of psychoanalytic inquiry in theoretical, philosophical, applied, and clinical psychoanalysis. Its aims are broadly academic, interdisciplinary, and pluralistic, emphasizing secularism and tolerance across the psychoanalytic domain. CPS aims to promote open and inclusive dialogue among the humanities and the social-behavioral sciences including such disciplines as philosophy, anthropology, history, literature, religion, cultural studies, sociology, feminism, gender studies, political thought, moral psychology, art, drama, and film, biography, law, economics, biology, and cognitive-neuroscience.

Of Philosophers and Madmen
A disclosure of Martin Heidegger, Medard Boss, and Sigmund Freud

Richard Askay and Jensen Farquhar

Amsterdam - New York, NY 2011

Cover illustration: The book cover is derived from an original oil painting entitled, "Listening-in" by Jensen Farquhar. It is a portrait of Dr. Medard Boss with Martin Heidegger's profile composing his right ear, and Sigmund Freud's profile as his left ear. The metaphorical significance of this painting represents Boss's struggle to synthesize the theories of Heidegger and Freud in order to create a new therapy, Daseinsanalysis.

Cover Design: Studio Pollmann

The paper on which this book is printed meets the requirements of "ISO 9706:1994, Information and documentation - Paper for documents - Requirements for permanence".

ISBN: 978-90-420-3426-6
E-Book ISBN: 978-94-012-0714-0
© Editions Rodopi B.V., Amsterdam - New York, NY 2011
Printed in the Netherlands

Contents

Foreword

Collaborative projects by philosophy and psychotherapists are infrequent occurrences in the world of academe. It is such however that awaits the reader in the text that follows, twin halves of an august event, textured by extensive scholarly research and critical analyses by the philosopher Richard Askay and the therapist and philosopher Jensie Farquhar. Their interdisciplinary accomplishments across the two disciplines of philosophy and psychotherapy are not of an unknown quantity. In their award-winning book published in 2006, *Apprehending the Inaccessible: Freudian Psychoanalysis and Existential Phenomenology*, they already marked out new directions across the two disciplines.

That which makes their current project of particular interest is that it begins with a play in which the story line is that of an imaginary construct of a dialogue between Martin Heidegger and Sigmund Freud. Straightway the mind of the reader recalls the role and function of plays within a narrative to provide a more encompassing sub-text. Shakespeare's *Hamlet* specifically comes to mind "The play's the thing," announces Hamlet, proclaiming that its principal aim is "to catch the conscience of the King." In the play assembled by Askay and Farquhar, however, the aim of the play within their wider narrative is to catch the twists and turns in the confrontation of Freud's psychoanalysis with Heidegger's existential philosophy.

The narrative that follows addresses the central issues in the development of the encounter of both Freud's metapsychological theory and his guides for therapeutic practice with Heidegger's early philosophy, Medard Boss's Daseinsanalysis, and Ludwig Binswanger's phenomenological psychiatry.

Of Philosophers and Madmen contributes a fresh perspective on the theory and practice of psychotherapy as it marks out certain implications of philosophical analysis for the medical profession and for the future of the human sciences more generally.

Calvin O. Schrag
George Ade Distinguished Professor of Philosophy, Emeritus
Purdue University, West Lafayette Indiana

Preface

In the fall of 2009, the North Pacific Institute for Analytical Psychology (The Northwest Alliance for Psychoanalytic Study) invited us to write a play for their institute involving a dialogue between two of the greatest thinkers of the twentieth century, Martin Heidegger and Sigmund Freud. Since the two never met, we began to ponder an intriguing historical context in which both could express their respective ideas as well as their engagement. It did not escape our attention that Heidegger had been institutionalized for mental exhaustion, nor were we unaware that his initial encounters with Medard Boss occurred around that same time period. Boss provided us with the perfect catalyst to bring Heidegger and Freud together in a world of fantasy and fiction.

Our acquaintanceship with Boss was not only through his work. In 1986, we were visiting Europe on a grant we had received to research the relationship between phenomenology and psychoanalysis. While there, we were fortunate to have the opportunity to meet with Boss in his home, and to experience for ourselves the historical setting in which the Zollikon seminars had been conducted. The actual Zollikon seminars consisted of a series of lectures given between the years of 1959-1969 by Heidegger to various medical professionals, in hopes of facilitating a new way of seeing and thinking. Boss had kept the room intact, almost like a museum, and he sat before us, reminiscing about the days of the seminars, and his fond relationship with Heidegger, giving us an actual glimpse into an amazing historical past that came alive through his descriptions. It was then that Boss revealed his intention to publish the German edition of the *Zollikoner Seminare* that following year. This, of course, sparked our interest, and we discussed the possibility of Richard Askay pairing with our Austrian friend and colleague, Dr. Franz Mayr (who is also a Heideggerian expert) to translate the *Zollikon Seminars* into English. This prospect greatly pleased Boss who was interested in expanding his audience. Hence, our initial contact was an exciting, mutually bonding, and productive experience.

With the translation of the *Zollikon Seminars* underway, we engaged in correspondence with Boss through the mail. In the fall of 1989, Boss visited us in our home in Portland Oregon. He had recently gone to the University of California, Berkeley to give a lecture on Heidegger's philosophy on psychoanalysis, and we asked if he would deliver a special lecture on Dream Analysis for us at the University of Portland. He was more than happy to oblige. We had the opportunity to spend several days with him and his wife. During that time, we discussed many issues, including Boss' opinion of Carl Jung and Sigmund Freud. Having been an analysand of Freud's we were able to glean a more personal assessment of the man. Boss stressed to us that Freud the theorist was nothing like the warm, gentle therapist who had given him his lunch money on numerous occasions. Consistent with his therapeutic advice, Freud insisted that his analysands should pay a high cost for therapy— to secure the psychological value of the process. Yet being aware of the monetary challenges students faced, he would often offer Boss money after their sessions so he could afford to eat. This exemplified Freud's admirable character, and Boss never forgot his kindness. However, Boss was also clear that he never fully embraced Freud's metapsychology. His loyalties were unequivocally devoted to Heidegger, a man whom he greatly admired and offered nothing but accolades on his behalf. When we asked if he had ever disagreed with Heidegger, Boss was quite clear that he placed himself far below such a "great genius," and would never think to challenge him.

Both of us found Boss to be a very gracious man, thoughtful and committed to those he held in high esteem. He also disputed those with whom he disagreed, and was unmistakably opposed to both Jung's and Freud's philosophical approach to human beings. He considered, for instance, Jung's archetypes and collective unconscious to be an absurd theory, peppered with mistakes, and fundamentally misguided in its view of human beings. Similarly, he rejected Freud, not only in terms of his metapsychological theory, but also in relation to certain aspects of his therapeutic approach. For example, he believed that counter-transference was an artificial imposition on the therapeutic relationship. It was ridiculous, in his opinion, not to consider the therapeutic relationship a genuine relatedness between human beings, and he revealed to us that he had met his second wife when she was his analysand. She had sought her training under Boss, and was a Daseinsanalyst in her own right.

Regrettably, Boss died in 1990. After his death, political circumstances conspired to delay the publication of the *Zollikon Seminars* for another 10 years. Sadly, Boss never had the opportunity to see the final results of our mutual efforts. His support and encouragement on our behalf was sorely missed. Although it is doubtful that Boss would have approved of the great liberties taken in writing this fictitious account of a meeting among such remarkable thinkers, we do so respectfully and with immense admiration for all involved. This play is in honor of Dr. Medard Boss, the man who had faith in our abilities, and to whom we owe an immense debt.

The authors would like to acknowledge the North Pacific Institute for Analytical Psychology for their request for a play illustrating the intersections between Martin Heidegger and Sigmund Freud. A special thanks to Elizabeth Clark-Stern and Robin McCoy for their interest in our work, and for bringing the play *Of Philosophers and Madmen* into the realm of entertainment. We also want to acknowledge the actors, Michael Horne, Robert Bergman, and Tim Nelson who were exceptionally good at portraying our beloved characters; their performances were inspirational. Franz Mayr is also an important contributor to this book, lending us advice and suggestions regarding German culture and philosophy. In addition, we deeply appreciate our family members, especially Elizabeth Bryan and our children Søren, Emerson, and William Tyler. Their support is essential. In particular, it was William's brilliant formatting and editing skills that made this work possible.

Introduction

In the spring of 1946, Martin Heidegger—arguably the greatest philosopher of the twentieth century—suffered a mental breakdown while undergoing interrogations by the denazification commission regarding the nature and extent of his participation in the National Socialist Party during WWII. He was promptly taken to the Haus Baden Sanatorium for therapeutic treatment with the trained psychoanalyst, Dr. Viktor von Gebsattel. Here, for the first time in Heidegger's life, a concrete situation arose which was flush with opportunities for the immediate engagement of phenomenological[1] philosophy with psychoanalysis: phenomenological philosophy could show what it has to offer the psychotherapeutic context and psychoanalytic theory. Reciprocally—and this Heidegger was not necessarily prepared to see—psychoanalysis could show in a concrete situation what it has to offer philosophy. Before this event, Heidegger had had very little to say about psychoanalysis.

Little is known of the specific details of what happened in Heidegger's therapeutic sessions with Gebsattel. Heidegger's own account affords at best only a superficial glimpse. Heidegger recounts: "And what did he do? He took me on a hike up through the forest in the snow. That was all. But he showed me human warmth and friendship. Three weeks later I came back a healthy man again."[2] Presumably that was not all. Hugo Ott observed, "It was during this stay, incidentally, that the foundations were laid—or strengthened—for his subsequent close collaboration with a particular school of psychiatry, namely the existential—anthropological school of Ludwig Binswanger and Medard Boss, to which Gebsattel also subscribed."[3] What we do know is that in a letter of 1947, Heidegger mentions his discussion of "many questions concerning the philosophical foundations of psychotherapy" with Gebsattel.[4] It is unclear whether these discussions occurred during Heidegger's treatment at the sanatorium or in the months following.

---

[1] It is not entirely accurate to refer to Heidegger's philosophy as "phenomenology"—more precisely Heidegger developed his particular form of "phenomenological ontology." However, at times we use the broader title of "phenomenology" for simplicity's sake and ease of reading.

[2] Heinrich Petzet, *Encounters and Dialogues with Martin Heidegger 1929-1976*, trans. Parvis Emad and Kenneth Maly (Chicago: University of Chicago Press, 1993), 52.

[3] Hugo Ott, *Martin Heidegger: A Political Life*, trans. A. Blunden (London: Basic Books, 1993.), 346. Ott does not offer any specific details as to what he meant here.

[4] Martin Heidegger, *Zollikon Seminars: Protocols—Conversations—Letters*, edit. Medard Boss, trans. Franz Mayr and Richard Askay (Evanston, Ill.: Northwestern University Press, 2001), 238.

Given this set of historical circumstances, ineluctable and tantalizing questions emerge; one cannot help but wonder what it was like in those therapeutic sessions. What would it have been like for Heidegger to be a patient, that is, an analysand? Reciprocally, what would it have been like for a trained psychoanalyst to have a world-renowned philosopher as his analysand?

Fortunately, it is unnecessary for us to remain completely in the dark in our wonderment. Dr. Medard Boss, a trained psychoanalyst, friend and colleague of Heidegger's, wrote a book entitled, *Psychoanalysis and Daseinsanalysis*, in which he offers a detailed account of a patient—"Dr. Cobling"—who taught him to "see and think differently."[5] Interestingly, this patient shared many characteristics with Heidegger's own past and concerns. For instance, Dr. Cobling and Heidegger both suffered the constraints of a religious upbringing, and had endured "repeated depressive episodes" since youth;[6] both were fortunate to have "exceptional intelligence,"[7] and had successfully worked their way up to important positions in teaching institutions; both experienced a total collapse from external pressures, and were concerned about constant surveillance from the "spies." And both had issues regarding sexuality and its cultural engagement. For Dr. Cobling, the focus was on judgments from the "church ladies" for her apparent promiscuous behavior. For Heidegger, we speculate that his affair with his young student, Hannah Arendt, may have created problems in his home life, and potentially with university and church authorities. It likely did not help matters that Arendt was Jewish and underwent persecution for her ethnicity during WWII, nor that Heidegger's wife was a blatant anti-Semite,[8] and Heidegger himself an official member of the National Socialist Party. We speculate that these forces and stressful conditions may have contributed to his mental collapse shortly after the war.

It is also fortunate for our suppositions that Dr. Cobling, was quite challenging of traditional psychiatry, something Heidegger is well known for as well. Boss' traditional methods did not work because Dr. Cobling rejected the entire scientific application to human meaning, including notions of consciousness and unconsciousness. At one point, she insisted that psychiatrists had no knowledge of "reality," and was furious for Boss' total disregard for her immediate experiences, which he deemed "purely fictitious and hallucinatory."[9] Interesting, Dr. Cobling later revealed how Boss had

---

[5] Medard Boss, *Psychoanalysis and Daseinsanalysis*, trans. Ludwig Lefebre (New York: Dacapo Press, 1982), 5-27.

[6] Ibid., 5. Heidegger's depression was of great concern to his wife and his lover, Hannah Arendt. See Hannah Arendt and Martin Heidegger, *Letters 1925-1975*, ed. Ursula Ludz, trans. Andrew Shields (New York: Harcourt, 2004).

[7] Ibid.

[8] Ott, *Martin Heidegger*, 137-38; see also Rüdiger Safranski, *Martin Heidegger: Between Good and Evil*, trans. Ewald Osers (Cambridge: Harvard University Press, 1998), 378.

[9] Boss, *Psychoanalysis and Daseinsanalysis*, 10.

cured her. She said, "The faith in you gave me the courage *to settle down inwardly to the very ground of my existence*."[10] Boss wrote that he would have been "completely at a loss with this case if the Daseinsanalytic understanding of man had not come to his aid just in time."[11] Fortunately, Heidegger's philosophy provided Boss with precisely the description of human existence that he needed to cure his analysand. We can imagine, then, a therapeutic situation where "Professor Heidegger" performs his role as patient and teacher to our newly evolving "Dr. Boss." Indeed, Heidegger's actual therapist, Dr. Gebsattel, was also interested in transcending traditional Freudian psychoanalysis in hopes of developing a more humanistic therapy. It is not such an extraordinary leap, then, to conjecture what this therapeutic encounter might have been like.

The intention of this text is to offer an informative, and entertaining account of Heidegger's early philosophy, and its engagement with Freudian psychoanalysis. The authors' do not purport to "choose sides," or make any judgments regarding who holds the most adequate account of human existence, but rather to present both worldviews in such a way as to facilitate a dialogue among readers.

The book is divided into two sections: *Part One* of this text includes a fictional play in which Boss assumes the role of Heidegger's therapist in the Haus Baden Sanatorium. Boss provides the perfect catalyst to illustrate a concrete and theoretical engagement of psychoanalysis and Heidegger's philosophy. Through Boss, we demonstrate what each orientation has to offer the other. Indeed, in the play itself, we witness Boss' evolution from a more traditional psychoanalytic orientation to a phenomenological one. Boss also existentially manifests the personal stress of being caught between two giants—Heidegger and Freud—both of whom offers powerful albeit mutually conflicting insights.

It is also through Boss—a former analysand to Freud—that Freud's various opinions are able to surface. For instance, Freud's interest in philosophy is best described as ambivalent, and certainly did not encapsulate a phenomenological perspective. This is obvious from his relationship with Ludwig Binswanger who was interested in and influenced by both Husserlian and Heideggerian phenomenology, and shared some of his writings with Freud. Although Freud and Binswanger enjoyed a lifelong friendship, neither was able to appreciate fully the philosophical worldview of the other. In fact, Freud had little to say in regards to phenomenology; it appears that his

---

[10] Ibid., 27.
[11] Ibid., 26.

philosophical interest ended with traditional metaphysics, and only included a modest selection within that range.[12]

On the other hand, Heidegger had a great deal to say regarding Freudian psychoanalysis later in his philosophical career. Heidegger sensed a great catastrophe due to the inappropriate application of science to human existence, and compared it to the "new religion"—one that had potential for a disastrous impact on human relatedness. One of his primary reasons for participating in the Zollikon seminars was to try and mitigate the impact of this assault against humanity. Thus, the *Zollikon Seminars* provides a valuable resource for expressing Heidegger's attitude toward psychoanalysis. It also represents a collaborative effort on the part of both Heidegger and Boss to bring Heidegger's philosophy into the realm of medicine, creating a new grounding for Freudian psychoanalysis. This process involved both a rejection of Freudian metapsychology, and a new approach to therapy that incorporated the philosophical ideas of Heidegger's early philosophy. Hence, this text includes an actual "demonstration" of how participants might have reacted to one another—had they been in direct contact—as well as discussions on a variety of relevant philosophical-historical topics.

With all the criticisms from the phenomenological perspective launched against Freud's psychoanalysis—particularly Freud's application of the scientific methodology in the development of his metapsychology—the authors are also interested in giving "Freud" an opportunity to respond directly to his assailants. Fortunately, Freud's work is rich in defense, having undergone assaults from both the philosophical and scientific communities during his own lifetime. Hence, the authors make use of Freud's specific arguments as well as his particular philosophical perspective, taken to some extent from the philosophy of Arthur Schopenhauer. As a medium between Freud and Heidegger, Boss' character provides the opportunity to explore Freud's attitude toward philosophy as well as some of the challenges he faced during his formulation and defense of psychoanalysis. Actual quotes from Heidegger's, Freud's, and Boss' works have been used whenever possible, and footnotes are provided for those who are interested in further investigation. Although the words and ideas of these important figures have been taken out of context, allowing the participants to "speak for themselves" contributes to the play's historical accuracy and appeal.

Part Two of this text explores the basic philosophical-psychological perspectives of the primary figures involved in a dialogue between Heidegger and Freud as well as a general discussion on philosophy and madness. We begin with a brief overview of Freud's psychoanalysis for those who are unfamiliar with the basic tenets of his ideas. In contrast, Heidegger's phenomenological approach in his early philosophy is included. Here the

---

[12] See Richard Askay, and Jensen Farquhar, *Apprehending the Inaccessible: Freudian Psychoanalysis and Existential Phenomenology* (Evanston: Northwestern University Press, 2006) for an extensive discussion on Freud's philosophical heritage.

authors situate readers in an actual concrete phenomenological scenario, and ask them to consider and respond to questions that might naturally emerge. Hence, while reading there is a direct demonstration and engagement with Heidegger's "new way of thinking and seeing."

We then present readers with an overall critique of Freudian psychoanalysis from a Heideggerian perspective. Ludwig Binswanger and Medard Boss are also specifically included in Part II because of their reactions against Freudian psychoanalysis, and their attempts to provide an alternative therapy. Both had personal and professional ties to Heidegger and Freud, and represent the emergence of a new psychoanalysis—that came to be known as Daseinsanalysis—grounded in Heideggerian phenomenological ontology.

In the final chapter of this text, we briefly explore the issue of madness as it relates to philosophers, most specifically Heidegger, and consider what Freudian psychoanalysis and Heideggerian phenomenology have to offer one another towards a holistic understanding of human suffering.

Hence, Part II of this text is intended to provide readers with a glimpse into the basic theories that emerged during this intriguing fragment of human history, one that is flush with intellectual struggles to comprehend how humans actually *are* in the world—how they think, live, toil, and suffer. Despite their differences in perspectives, each offers interesting insights toward a deeper understanding of human existence.

It should be mentioned that the chosen title for this book, *Of Philosophers and Madmen*, corresponds to John Steinbeck's *Of Mice and Men*, suggesting the smallest and greatest of human potential. It also refers to that thin line between genius and madness that is alluded to throughout the history of ideas, and remains an ambiguous—and, at times, blatant—issue for many great thinkers. In situating Heidegger in the Haus Baden Sanatorium, we witness him in a moment of weakness *and* strength. Heidegger's ability to defend himself against the attacks of his own vulnerability demonstrates powerful aspects of his philosophy as well as pertinent applications of both Freudian psychoanalysis and Boss' Daseinsanalysis. There is no doubt that this historical event—a merging of philosopher and madman—gave Heidegger direct experience for a philosophical perspective that significantly impacted the history of psychoanalysis.

PART I

Of Philosophers and Madmen: A Play

Cast of Characters

DR. MEDARD BOSS, a forty four-year-old Swiss psychoanalyst who was an analysand (i.e., patient) of Sigmund Freud's when he was a student in Vienna. He is also a friend and colleague to Dr. Ludwig Binswanger—a psychoanalyst, and mutual friend of both Sigmund Freud and Martin Heidegger—and thus provides the ideal medium for a dialogue between Freud and Heidegger. Boss wears a doctor's coat over a suit and tie from the mid-1940s. He often carries a clipboard, and always carries a pen and notepad in his breast pocket.

DR. SIGMUND FREUD, an apparition of Medard Boss' who appears as his alter ego to provide both insight into the psyche of Boss' analysand, Martin Heidegger, and pertinent information regarding Freudian psychoanalysis. Although dead, "Freud" appears to be in his mid to late sixties—the age he would have been when he was Boss' analyst. He has a beard, reading glasses, and wears a pocket-watch; he is dressed in a suit and tie, appropriate for the late 1920's—early 1930's, and is often seen with a cigar in his hand. He carries a pen and notepad in his breast pocket.

DR. MARTIN HEIDEGGER, a famous German philosopher in his mid-to-late fifties who has suffered a mental collapse after the denazification hearings in 1946. He is considered brilliant, but paranoid. He suffers from bouts of depression as well as auditory and visual hallucinations. He sports a small mustache ("Hitler" style), and wears a slightly disheveled white shirt, suit and tie, appropriate for the year 1946.

DOCTOR(S), at the sanatorium. He wears a white doctor's coat over a suit and tie, and carries a clipboard.

Play Setting

The play takes place in 1946, at the Haus Baden Sanitorium in Badenweiler, Germany. The entire play can be performed without set changes, if it is constructed in a minimalist fashion. There is a large sign with the name of the sanatorium—"Haus Baden Sanatorium,"—across the top of the stage. The stage is divided into two rooms, with a narrow hallway running between the two. To the right is Heidegger's room, demarcated by a doorframe with the words, "Hermeneutical Phenomenological Ontology"—representing Heidegger's philosophy—located above the door. The room itself is sparse, containing only a cot with a night table beside it, an extra chair by the door, a desk with a chair, a place where Heidegger's coat and hat hang, as well as an umbrella in an umbrella stand. To the left of the stage is Dr. Boss' office. It too is demarcated with a doorframe. Above the door is a sign that reads, "Psychoanalysis." In the office is a couch, a chair that is off to the side and in the position of "therapist" to the couch, a table with decanters of alcohol and drinking glasses, a desk—with a photo of Sigmund Freud—and chair, and a briefcase next to the desk (containing a picture of Heidegger with Boss). A small space to accommodate the two actors on "a walk" should be left at the front of the stage. Lighting is used to focus the audience's attention on the appropriate events during the scenes.

If an intermission is desired, it naturally occurs after Act II, Scene 2.

Of Philosophers and Madmen

ACT I

SCENE 1:   DOCTORS are gathered in the halls of the Haus Baden Sanitorium,[1] discussing the new patient, Martin Heidegger. DR. MEDARD BOSS[2] is among them. BOSS is holding a clipboard in his hand that also contains a "chart." On top of his clipboard is a book—Sigmund Freud's *Papers on Metapsychology*.[3] BOSS has a pen and small notepad in his breast pocket.

Doctor: (To Boss.) It appears that we have the great philosopher Professor Heidegger in our sanatorium. He was brought here last night, by Doktor Beringer[4] after suffering from a mental breakdown during his interrogation before the denazification commission. Doktor Binswanger[5] has suggested that you take his case, since you ostensibly have some interest in his philosophy.

Boss: (Looking through notes on his clipboard.) Yes, of course. It is a privilege. I have wanted to meet Professor Heidegger for some time now. From what I gather, his work is most impressive. Doktor Binswanger believes that he is our new savior…his ideas have much to offer psychoanalysis.

Doctor: (Smiling.)   Well, we shall see.   Right now, I suspect our psychoanalysis is more in a position to help him than his own philosophy can help us, or even himself…

---

[1] The Haus Baden Sanatorium in Badenweiler is where Heidegger received medical attention for his mental breakdown after the denazification hearings in 1946. Safranski, *Martin Heidegger*, 351.

[2] There is no concrete evidence that Medard Boss was Heidegger's analyst. Although the exact date of their first meeting is unclear, Boss had contact with Heidegger near the time that Heidegger had his mental breakdown. Boss was closely involved with Heidegger's philosophy, and they developed a close friendship from which Daseinsanalysis evolved. Heidegger, *Zollikon Seminars*, vii-xxi.

[3] Sigmund Freud, *The Complete Psychological Works of Sigmund Freud*, Vol XIV, trans by James Strachey (London: The Hogarth Press, 1957). Citations from the Standard Edition (hereafter abbreviated as *SE*) are by volume and page number.

[4] Doctor Beringer was the dean of the medical school at the University of Freiburg who was present with Heidegger before the denazification commission. He was responsible for taking Heidegger to the Haus Baden Sanatorium. (Safranski, *Martin Heidegger*, 352).

[5] Freud also discussed the proper length of time for therapeutic session. Sessions were typically 50 minutes long, allowing for 10-minute intervals in-between patients.

Boss: (Looks up from his notes.) All right then, I shall go meet the great professor. Thank you, doctor. (Boss begins to walk away.)

Doctor: (Calls after Boss.) A lot of good his philosophy has done him lately…He can barely function in his current state…

(Boss proceeds to Heidegger's room, carrying a clipboard. He opens the door of the room where Heidegger is seated on a cot in darkness. The light from the hallway shines on him. Boss goes to turn on the room light and Heidegger flinches. Boss dims the light. He walks over to Heidegger to introduce himself.)

Boss: (Confident and bold.) Good day, Herr Professor Heidegger. My name is Doktor Boss. (Boss extends his hand. Heidegger hunches over and covers his ears. Boss clears his throat.) I have heard a great deal about your work, and I must say it is an honor to be assigned to your case. (Heidegger is unresponsive.) It seems you have been having a difficult time of it lately.

Heidegger: (Unresponsive, still covering his ears.)

Boss: (Pulls a chair to the cot and sits down across from Heidegger.) I notice that you are covering your ears. Are there sounds that are unpleasant to you?

Heidegger: Noise, noise, noise! "I can't do anything else but hang on to every sound until it has died away…"[6]

Boss: What are the sounds saying to you?

Heidegger: (Says loudly.) GUILTY!

Boss: (Looking at his notes.) Are you referring to the interrogation?

Heidegger: "…the call 'says' *nothing* which might be talked about, gives no information about events…[it] comes *from* uncanniness."[7]

Boss: Do you hear voices? Is someone calling you?

Heidegger: "The caller is, to be sure, indefinite; but the 'whence' from which it calls does not remain a matter of indifference for the calling. This 'whence'…gets called too in the calling…it too gets disclosed."[8]

---

[6] Boss, Psychoanalysis and Daseinsanalysis, 6.
[7] Martin Heidegger, *Being and Time,* trans. John Macquarrie and E. Robinson (New York: Harper and Row, 1962), 325.
[8] Ibid.

Boss: (Looks confused.) What gets disclosed?

Heidegger: Thrownness. "The Self, which as such has to lay the basis for itself, can *never* get that basis into its power; and yet, as existing, it must take over Being-a-basis. To be its own thrown basis is that potentiality-for-Being which is the issue for care."[9]

Boss: Hmmm…I see…and how do you find yourself today?

Heidegger: I am not able to.

Boss: Able to what?

Heidegger: Find myself. Isn't that what you asked?

Boss: (Looks at his clipboard, thumbs through some of his papers. Writes some notes down on his pad. Looks at Heidegger.) Do you know where you are? Why you are here?

Heidegger: (Shakes head. Pause. Mumbles.) The door opened. The light illuminated the darkness, revealing the clearing…My presence, it holds open the possibilities…(Voice trails off.)

Boss: Excuse me?

Heidegger: It's all so "simple."

Boss: What is?

Heidegger: It no longer speaks to us.[10]

Boss: (Writing in his notes.) What no longer speaks? The voices?

Heidegger: No, no, no, no…(Pause.) Why are *they* treating me like this?

Boss: I'm sorry. Did the staff not show you your due respect, Herr Professor?

Heidegger: (Continuing and interrupting Boss.) My god, they are treating me like, like… Fritz…[11]

---

[9] Ibid., 330.

[10] Heidegger, *Zollikon Seminars*, 102.

[11] Here we are making reference to the philosophical proximity between Heidegger's "madness" and Friedrich Nietzsche's insanity. Heidegger had a fascination with

Boss: Fritz, you say? (Looking through his notes.) Do you mean your brother Fritz…(Voice trails off.)[12]

Heidegger: (Continues speaking as if Boss is not there.) Not only have *they* misunderstood and made use of my philosophy in precisely the same way…I'm utterly amazed that they haven't simply shipped me off to Weimar…since I am apparently Dionysus incarnate…[13]

Boss: Weimar? Have you spent time in Weimar? (Looks through notes.)

Heidegger: (Long pause. In suspicious tone.) It's undoubtedly because we both identified the history of metaphysics as nihilism.[14]

Boss: Nihilism, you say? Hmmm…Are you concerned that people consider you a nihilist?

Heidegger: (Laughs.) Concerned what THEY think? Absurd!

Boss: (Tentatively.) Are you a nihilist?

Heidegger: (Shakes head and looks at the floor.) "The nothing itself nihilates….In the Being of beings the nihilation of the nothing occurs…[Yet] we turn away from the nothing…[and] hasten into the public [superficialities] of existence."[15]

Boss: You have been through a lot, Herr Professor. But I do believe that all of us here can help you. Talk to me…I am listening very carefully to what you're saying!

Heidegger: (Shaking his head.) No, you don't understand. Only he who already understands can listen.[16]

Nietzsche's work, and wrote four volumes on his philosophy. Martin Heidegger, *Nietzsche,* vols. 1-4, trans. David Krell (San Francisco: Harper and Row, 1984).
[12] Heidegger coincidentally had a brother named Fritz. Safranski, *Martin Heidegger*, 7.
[13] Nietzsche was taken to Weimar after his mental collapse. Rüdiger Safranski, *Nietzsche: A Philosophical Biography,* trans. Shelley Frisch (New York, NY: Norton and Company, 2002), 318, 337. In his madness (and in his work, *Ecco Homo*), Nietzsche refers to himself as Dionysus (Ibid., 344).
[14] It is a common misunderstanding of both Nietzsche's and Heidegger's philosophies that they lead to nihilism. Instead, they offer a critique of nihilism. Martin Heidegger, *Nietzsche,* vols. 1 & 2, 151 ff.
[15] Martin Heidegger, *Basic Writings,* edit. David Krell (New York: Harper and Row, 1977), 105-6.
[16] Heidegger, *Being and Time,* 207.

Boss: (Look of concern.) OK, so help me understand. You are safe now. You can tell me anything. No one will harm you here.

Heidegger: There is no foundation to our very being and yet we demand one…this is the burden of our existence.[17]

Boss: Does your life seem a burden to you?

Heidegger: I "do not evade the silent voice that attunes me toward the horror of the abyss."[18] (Looking down at his hands.) There are times when I drift "here and there in the abysses of our existence like a muffling fog."[19] "During [these] darker times, I hardly know anymore who and where I am. None of us knows that, as soon as we stop fooling ourselves."[20]

Boss: (Concerned.) Yes, well you have suffered a mental breakdown. It isn't unusual for a person to feel a bit…lost…after undergoing such traumatic events…

Heidegger: (Obviously feeling ill at ease, dazed, and yet peculiarly calm.) I feel anxious…my world has collapsed, it utterly lacks significance.[21] All things and I myself have sunk in indifference…I can get no hold on things…there is the slipping away of beings as a whole…I am slipping away from myself.[22] There is only naked strangeness.[23]

Boss: (Leans forward in his chair, trying hard to understand.) What are you anxious about?

Heidegger: Nothing…its breath perpetually quivers through me,[24] and yet it also "…takes [my] breath away."[25] (Both remain silent for a moment. Heidegger looks suspiciously at Boss.) Silence is a particular way of expressing yourself about something to me.[26]…Ah, but what is your silence

---

[17] Ibid., 329-30.
[18] Martin Heidegger, *Pathmarks*, trans. William McNeil (Cambridge: Cambridge University Press, 1998), 233.
[19] Heidegger, *Basic Writings*, 101.
[20] Martin Heidegger, *Discourse On Thinking*, trans. John M. Anderson and E. Hans Freund (Evanston: Harper & Row, 1966), 44-45.
[21] Heidegger, *Being and Time*, 231.
[22] Heidegger, *Basic Writings*, 103; see also *Being and Time*, 232.
[23] Heidegger, *Being and Time*, 394.
[24] Heidegger, *Basic Writings*, 108.
[25] Martin Heidegger, *History of the Concept of Time: Prolegomena*, trans. Theodore Kisiel (Bloomington: Indiana University Press, 1985), 290.
[26] Ibid., 267.

concealing? Is it perhaps "...the soundlessness of uncanniness?"[27] Am I making you uncomfortable?

Boss: (Stumbling.) No, not at all, I'm just trying to understand what has happened.

Heidegger: (Shakes his head and sighs.) What has happened is that I am no longer at home with myself.[28]

Boss: Oh, I see. This is an unfamiliar place to be sure. Of course you feel a bit disoriented. But, it is important that you feel at home here for the time being. Are there, perhaps, some things that your wife could bring you to help you feel more at home? (Looks around the room.) I dare say this room could use a little sprucing up.

Heidegger: "A human being's limited belonging to the realm of the unconcealed constitutes his being a self...[and] a human being who adjusts to the limits [of a given situation is]...thus, at home with himself, is *Himself*."[29]

Boss: Yes, well I suspect that in time you will adjust to being here. We are all here to help you adjust.

Heidegger: (Looks directly at Boss.) *Who* is it that you are trying to help? Now, be careful, the answer may not be as obvious as you think. The "who" of everyday existence may not be me at all.

Boss: (Writing in his note pad.) That's partly what we are here to discover...(Looks at Heidegger) to help you discover...who exactly you are...

Heidegger: (Frustrated, shaking his head.) I am not a substantial subject or thing.[30] I have no permanent essence that constitutes my core nature...I am merely a way of existing[31]...a "happening" in the process of realizing itself.[32]

Boss: Yes, well it is your *way* of existing lately that concerns us. We need to figure out what went wrong, what led to this recent mental collapse...help you

---

[27] Heidegger, *Being and Time*, 343.
[28] Ibid., 233.
[29] Heidegger, *Zollikon Seminars*, 188.
[30] Martin Heidegger, *The Basic Problems of Phenomenology,* trans. Albert Hofstadter (Bloomington: Indiana University Press, 1982), 169; see also Heidegger, *Zollikon Seminars*, 174.
[31] Heidegger, *Being and Time*, 153, 312, 365, 369.
[32] Martin Heidegger, *The Metaphysical Foundations of Logic,* trans. Michael Heim (Bloomington: Indiana University Press, 1984), 139.

find more effective ways of coping…(Looking with concern at Heidegger)…help you reconstruct yourself…

Heidegger: (Silent for a bit. Shaking head.) It is the nothing that makes selfhood possible. The nothing makes possible my "who."[33]

Boss: (Confused.) What did you say? The nothing?

Heidegger: (In an insistent and yet, resigned tone.) Nothing matters. Nothing matters. Nothing matters. (Continues saying this while Boss talks to him.)

Boss: Surely something matters to you! What about your family, Herr Professor? (Looks at notes.) Your wife is waiting for you in Freiburg. Have you spoken to her recently?

Heidegger: (Shaking head.) Nothing matters…nothing matters…

Boss: (Stops looking through his papers and looks at Heidegger.) Nothing matters?

Heidegger: (Loud voice.) NO, doctor! (Pause.) Nothing MATTERS. We must ponder the nothing.

Boss: We must ponder the nothing? Why is this, Herr Professor?

Heidegger: "Only on the ground of wonder—the revelation of the nothing— does the 'why?' loom before us."[34] Nothing discloses the nullity that determines Dasein in its ground.[35] We have forgotten all that is dark and enigmatic in existence. The "inaccessible is the mystery."[36]

Boss: Dasein you say? Dasein means "being there," does it not?

Heidegger: Dasein! (Points to Boss.) You Herr Doktor. (Puts hands on his own chest.) Me, Herr Doktor. We are Dasein…always "here" yet always already our past, present, and future possibilities.

Boss: So Dasein means "human being?"

Heidegger: Why must you say "human being?" Why not lantern? (Points up at the ceiling.) Or light? (Sweeps hands through the air in the room.) Or

---

[33] Heidegger, *Basic Writings*, 106.
[34] Ibid., 111.
[35] Heidegger, *Being and Time*, 321f.
[36] Heidegger, *Zollikon Seminars*, 183.

illumination of the concealed? Don't tell me what is human. How can you know this? How can anyone know without first asking, "What does it mean to *be* as a human?" (Looks down and mutters.) That is the question… "…sometimes one *understands* one's subject matter, but in a darker moment, one no longer *sees* it."[37]

Boss: (Quizzically.) What *does* it mean to be as a human, Herr Professor?

Heidegger: (Looks up at Boss expectantly. Shows some excitement that Boss might be "getting it.") Precisely!

Boss: (Boss smiles and looks at Heidegger. But since Heidegger doesn't respond with an answer, and fearing that he will lose this initial contact, he asks again.) Well, what does it mean to be as a human? (Boss looks intently at Heidegger.)

Heidegger: (Less enthusiastically now.) Exactly. (Heidegger breaks eye contact and looks down again.)

Boss: (Looks at Heidegger with concern. He puts his hand over his chin and on his mouth, thinking of what to say next. Awkward silence.)

Boss: (In a rational tone.) As I've said, what you are experiencing is a mental collapse. The voices you hear, the images you see…they aren't real. You are experiencing hallucinations as a result of "a disturbed metabolism in the brain tissues."[38] (Stands up, pulls out a chart and holds it up for Heidegger to see). If you look here, (points to the chart) you can see from these "very agitated curves of [your] electroencephalogram" that your brain is not functioning properly.[39]

Heidegger: (Laughing.) "As though…a single human perception or thought— be it usual or unusual—could ever be intelligibly derived from the physiological processes of the bodily metabolism, from any nerve functions, or from the so-called higher nervous activities which take place concomitantly."[40] Tell me, Herr Doktor; are there also molecules of sorrow when one weeps?[41] When one departs from another, have these tears magically become "farewell" molecules?[42]

---

[37] Ibid., 29.
[38] Boss, *Psychoanalysis and Daseinsanalysis*, 8-9.
[39] Ibid., 9.
[40] Ibid.
[41] Heidegger, *Zollikon Seminars*, 7.
[42] Ibid., 155.

(Boss sits back down, shrinking in his chair. Looks very uncomfortable.)

Heidegger: (Continues contemptuously, sitting up straight now.) "How [do you]…picture such a transformation of physical processes into mental, immaterial phenomena? Perhaps as some kind of magic evaporation?"[43]

Boss: (Uncomfortable, but asserting his expertise.) "Not exactly that…Rather the physiological metabolism in the central nervous system and the mental phenomena might be regarded as two different aspects of one and the same thing. Whereas physiology approaches the functions of the central nervous system in terms of space and time, psychology approaches them in terms of various subjective phenomena, which are, however, only *the subjective reflections of physiological processes.*"[44]

(Heidegger shrugs and looks uninterested.)

Boss: (Assumes that Heidegger isn't getting it, takes the book of Freud's, stands up and hands it to Heidegger.) It's all here, if you want to learn more about the metapsychological foundations of psychoanalysis[45] …We know that subjective reflections…Well, they are much like "…reflection[s] of the light waves of an external object creating a picture on a photographic plate."[46]

Heidegger: (Looks at the book Boss handed him and scowls.) "Of which nature…would the cerebral cortex have to be in order that—as a material, organic tissue—it could enter into an understanding, meaning-disclosing relationship with the external world?…[W]hat should the physiological processes reflect themselves subjectively? Into the consciousness of a subject, perhaps? But what would the nature of such a subject have to be in order to be able to possess a consciousness? And would…[you] be kind enough to explain…what consciousness is and where [you] think the human consciousness would be found? Somewhere within the head, perhaps, or somewhere else?"[47]

Boss: (Sitting down again, stuttering a bit.) Well, I…consciousness…um…

---

[43] Boss, *Psychoanalysis and Daseinsanalysis*, 9.
[44] Ibid.
[45] The book "Boss" hands to "Heidegger" is the *Papers on Metapsychology* by Sigmund Freud (*SE* XIV). Boss did convince Heidegger to read a bit of Freud's theoretical and therapeutic works, however it is unclear which specific works Heidegger actually read. Heidegger's reaction to Freud's writing was not terribly positive, to say the least.
[46] Boss, *Psychoanalysis and Daseinsanalysis*, 9.
[47] Ibid.

Heidegger: "Was it perhaps this consciousness which [you] had just compared with a photographic plate?"[48]

Boss: Yes, well…

Heidegger: "…has a photographic plate ever been capable of perceiving that which was reflected on it as the thing which it was?"[49]

Boss: (Leans forward.)   Look, I didn't mean to imply that your "hallucinations [are] simply nothing…" I know that they seem perfectly real to you…I only meant to tell you that   "[t]hey d[o] not…correspond to an external reality, but represent only an internal, purely psychic reality, consisting of hidden emotions and tendencies…These internal psychic realities [are] being projected out of the deep unconscious layers of [your] psyche and on to external objects."[50]

Heidegger: (Furious now. Pushes the book away. Stands up. Paces.) "Don't you come with that psychological nonsense again, trying to make fictions of [my experience]…to dispose of them as mere hallucinations and projections of my unconscious or some other psychic reality. What do you psychiatrists know of reality anyway? Nothing, absolutely nothing! And then you go ahead and make tidy subdivisions of something about which you haven't the faintest inkling."[51]

Boss: (Shrinking in his chair.)

Heidegger: (Still pacing.) "You prattle about subjective and objective, about an inner, psychic reality and a real reality attaching to the external world, presuming to play one against the other, as though the one were real and the other purely fictitious and hallucinatory. But, what can you actually mean by the very word hallucination when you completely ignore what the so-called non-hallucinatory reality is?" (Flings hands in air.) "Words, nothing but words—and behind them nothing, precisely nothing, no real understanding whatsoever!"[52] Go now! JUST LET ME BE! No more of your tortuous words! Poof! Be gone with you!

Boss: (Looking shocked and very uncomfortable.) Yes, well…

THE LIGHTS DIM.

---

[48] Ibid.
[49] Ibid., 9-10.
[50] Ibid., 10.
[51] Ibid.
[52] Ibid.; see also Heidegger, *Zollikon Seminars*, 74.

[LIGHTS RISE again showing BOSS in his office at his desk reading *Being and Time.* At the same time, HEIDEGGER is in his room, sitting in a chair at his desk, and thumbing through Freud's *Metapsychology Papers.* HEIDEGGER looks irritated and angry. He reads a bit, shakes his head, stands up and paces, goes back to reading, looks frustrated...BOSS sits at his desk reading and looking confused.]

LIGHTS DIM to darkness on HEIDEGGER, but BOSS is still lit up. He is still reading *Being and Time.*

END OF SCENE

ACT I

SCENE 2: BOSS grows tired of reading *Being and Time*. He gets up from his desk and goes over to the couch. He lies down on a couch in his office.[53] As he drifts to sleep--lights dim to darkness and when lights come up again, BOSS is reclined on the couch and SIGMUND FREUD is sitting behind Boss in the position of "therapist" to Boss. FREUD is wearing glasses, and writing on a small notepad. In his jacket pocket, FREUD has some papers, and a pocket-watch.

Freud: (Looking at his note pad.) So you were saying that this patient of yours has brought you back to your days as a penurious student and my patient?[54]

Boss: (A bit surprised, stretches his neck to look at Freud.) Herr Doktor Freud? I thought you were dead![55]

Freud: Yes, well it seems that I am not dead to you, my friend. Obviously you still need me. But as you were saying...

Boss: (Lying comfortably.) Oh yes...it's this patient...so frustrating...

Freud: You have been feeling confused, perhaps? A bit out of your depth? Why do you think this is?

Boss: (In a low tone.) He mocks me...(Says defensively:) I am the expert, I am the one with extensive training in these matters...and yet, he mocks me. He laughs, and he scorns me, as though I'm an ignorant child.

Freud: (Writing in his note pad.) Hmmm....I see. You feel yourself a child being scolded for your bad behavior.

Boss: Yes! It's as though none of this has mattered, as though years of training never happened. I have no past, no future. I'm just this idiot of a child at the mercy of my superiors.

---

[53] For a variety of reasons, Freud believed that it was crucial for patients to lie on a couch while the therapist sat behind the patient during therapy, *SE* XII, 133-34; 139.

[54] Boss was actually an analysand of Freud's when he was a student in Vienna in 1925. This was revealed to the authors of this play during a visit with Dr. Boss at their home in 1989.

[55] Freud died in 1939; the play takes place in 1946. "Freud" serves as a therapeutic consultant to Boss in order to facilitate a dialogue between Heidegger and Freud. In actuality, Heidegger and Freud never met.

Freud: (Thumbing through his note pad.)...As you know, often times feelings of inferiority stem from a lack of love[56]...Your father...Remember how you often spoke to me of your father...

Boss: (In a child's voice, quiet.) He comes to me as this broken man...I am the authority...I can help him...but does he let me? No, he cannot see who I've become...

Freud: Who cannot see, your father or this patient of yours? Perhaps they are one and the same...?

Boss: If I could just show him that I am worthy...

Freud: If you could prove yourself to him...what then?

Boss: He would see me as I am...

Freud: As you want to be seen...

Boss: Yes, as I want to be seen...

Freud: I feel I must warn you, Herr Doktor...These feelings you are having...You can only take a patient as far as you yourself have gone[57]...

Boss: Yes, well my patient...he has gone so far in the world...A brilliant man...He is considered to be perhaps the greatest philosopher of our time...and I have this opportunity...

Freud: (Looking up from his notebook.)...Just don't allow your ambitions to hinder the therapeutic process...

Boss: No, of course...He is in my care, I must find a way to cure this Professor Heidegger...

Freud: Heidegger, you say? Hmmm...if I recall correctly our friend Doktor Binswanger worked with Professor Heidegger, did he not?

Boss: (Sitting up with interest, facing Freud.) Yes he did. Doktor Binswanger was responsible for sending Professor Heidegger to me.

Freud: Was he now...(Searching through his pockets.) It has been some time, but I seem to recall that Doktor Binswanger sent me a copy of his lecture on

---

[56] Freud, *SE* XXII, 65.

[57] Freud, *SE* XIV, 20.

Professor Heidegger…(Freud pulls out some papers from his jacket pocket, and looks at them.)   Here it is: "Freud's Conception of Man in Light of Anthropology." In it, Doktor Binswanger argues, "man is not only mechanical necessity…not merely in-the-world. His existence is understandable only as being-in-the-world, as the projection and disclosure of world—as Heidegger so powerfully demonstrated."[58]

Boss: Hmmm. What did you think of it?

Freud: (Still looking at the paper and shaking his head.) I'm afraid that my response was characteristically skeptical. (Looks up from the paper as though he is quoting himself.) "…I rejoiced over [Binswanger's] beautiful prose…the scope of [his] horizon, [his] tact in disagreement…(shakes head)…*But, of course, I don't believe a word of what [he said].*"[59]

Boss: (A little surprised.) Really?   What was it that you found so disagreeable?

Freud: (In a snide tone as he stuffs the paper back in his jacket pocket.) Well, what first occurred to me was to ponder the question, "What on earth could possibly compel a man to include such ubiquitous hyphens?" Really! Did you read that lecture?! All through the pages, he has words like Being-hyphen-in-hyphen-the-hyphen-world-hyphen-hyphen, and Being-hyphen-with-hyphen-hyphen, and Being-hyphen-hyphen-in?! (Gasps for air.) Seriously, was the man afflicted with a typographical stutter? (Shakes his head.)

Boss: (Chuckling.) I thought I was the only one who considered that a bit excessive.

Freud: "Personally, [I have] particular difficulty grasping such abstract ideas, ideas that should have been presented in a much more elementary manner."[60]

Boss: (Shakes head in agreement, and smiles.) At times, I wonder if philosophers don't intentionally make their ideas obscure, or pepper them with nonsense, so that one feels a sense of accomplishment—perhaps even superiority?—with the least little bit of insight.

---

[58] Ludwig Binswanger, *Being-in-the-World: Selected Papers of Ludwig Binswanger,* trans. Jacob Needleman (New York: Harper and Row, 1963), 169. Binswanger was a life-long friend of Freud's and a professional acquaintance of Heidegger's for several decades.
[59] Ibid., 4.
[60] Hermann Nunberg, and Ernst Federn (eds.), *Minutes of the Vienna Psychoanalytic Society,* vol. 2 trans. M. Nunberg (New York: International Universities Press, 1975), 335.

Freud: (Laughing.) "As if the most useless things in the world were not arranged in the following order: shirt collars, philosophers, and monarchs."[61]

(Both laugh together.)

Boss: (Says a bit more seriously.) But I seem to recall that you once spoke rather highly of philosophy.

Freud: (More serious.) Yes, well I have always been a bit ambivalent when it came to philosophy. (Pause. Leans back in his chair to reminisce, looking upward)...Early in my academic life, I believed that my original goal was to pursue philosophy because of the insight it afforded.[62] Indeed, it was under the influence of Professor Brentano—(Looks at Boss) an utterly brilliant man, by the way (Looks away again)—that I had decided to take my Ph.D. in philosophy and zoology.[63]

Boss: (Takes out a note pad from his shirt pocket and thumbs through it.) Hmmm. Very interesting. I believe it was Doktor Brentano's analysis of the different senses of Being in Aristotle's philosophy that served as a lightning bolt for Professor Heidegger's philosophy as well.[64]

Freud: (Not really paying attention to Boss while he continues to reminisce. Sighs.) "But philosophy has no direct influence on the great mass of mankind; it is of interest to only a small number even of the top layer of intellectuals and is scarcely intelligible to anyone else."[65] "I not only have no capability for philosophy, but no respect for it...in secret, I cannot say this aloud, I believe that metaphysics will one day be seen as a nuisance, as a misuse of thought...and it will be judged thus."[66] No, our primary task should be to translate metaphysics into metapsychology.[67] That is how we will solve the puzzle of human mental functioning.

Boss: (Taking notes, pauses and looks confused.) But is it not possible for philosophy to offer some grounding, some insight into the psychology of human beings...

---

[61] Walter Boehlich, ed., *The Letters of Sigmund Freud to Eduard Silberstein*, trans. Arnold Pomerans (Cambridge, Mass.: Belknap Press, 1990), 52.
[62] Sigmund Freud, *The Origins of Psychoanalysis: Letters to Willheilm Fliess,* trans. Eric Mosbacher and J. Strachey (New York: Basic Books, 1954), 141.
[63] Boehlich, *Letters of Sigmund Freud to Eduard Silberstein*, 95.
[64] Heidegger, *Zollikon Seminars*, 295.
[65] Freud *SE* XXII, 161.
[66] Sigmund Freud, *The Letters of Sigmund Freud,* ed., Ernst Freud, trans. Tania Stern and James Stern (New York: Basic Books, 1975), 375.
[67] Freud, *SE* VI, 259.

Freud: (Interrupting) Nonsense! Do not allow yourself to fall prey to the twisted thinking of philosophers…Philosophers may claim to provide the foundation for human existence, but even at its best, philosophy is only sublimation…a fine contribution to our society, perhaps, but nonetheless merely a form of defense against those most basic urges.

Boss: Yes, well psychoanalysis has undergone a great deal of attack from these superior intellectuals over the years…I can understand your frustrations…

Freud: Interesting how philosophers often make pronouncements against psychoanalysis and yet have rarely experienced therapy themselves, or studied the darker crevices of the human mind[68]…

Boss: So true! I must admit that I am curious about this Professor Heidegger…At last; I have the opportunity to explore in depth, the libidinal energies of a very powerful thinker…

Freud: (Shouts:) "Psychography!"

Boss: What's that, you say?

Freud: Psychography…it's an idea of mine…Psychoanalysis has a great deal to offer philosophy by examining the psychoanalytical underpinnings of the philosopher's ideas…(Boss writes this down on his notepad.) This is CRUCIAL. We both know that the conscious thinking of a philosopher is secretly guided and forced into certain channels by his instincts. No matter how much fuss he makes about his philosophical reflections, he must face up to his instinctual rootedness. And we psychoanalysts are the ideal archeologists to unearth the buried forces…to reveal the sources—what compels particular philosophers to generate specific worldviews, and why… "Psychoanalysis can indicate subjective and individual motives behind philosophical theories which have ostensibly sprung from impartial logical works. It enables us to better understand the meaning and origins of philosophical creations."[69]

Boss: (Looks up from his notepad.) Of course I agree with you…Did I mention that I gave Professor Heidegger a copy of your papers on metapsychology? He's quite resistant, of course. It took a great deal of

---

[68] Freud, *SE* XIX, 13. The primary exceptions to this during Freud's time were Schopenhauer and Nietzsche.
[69] Freud, *SE* XIII, 179.

"guile and cunning" on my part,[70] but I think he will read it and perhaps even understand what we are trying to do for him. I've been reading his book, *Being and Time*, and I must admit it is exceptional...(pause). (Says thoughtfully:) Of course, much of what he says—even when he's lucid—makes him sound like "a man from Mars...visiting earth-dwellers in an attempt to communicate with them."[71] (Shakes head.) It's hard to make sense of his work...

Freud: Hmmm. Tell me more of this Professor *Martian* Heidegger (Chuckling at his own joke.) How does he appear to you now?

Boss: Well, he only occasionally makes sense. I believe he has a disturbed metabolism of the brain tissues. He hears voices, hallucinates...He is a bit paranoid and quite depressed.

Freud: (Shaking his head in agreement.) Yes, this comes as no surprise to me. Many "neurotic brooder[s]...are found among the philosophers; they show traits that bear a particularly striking resemblance to the obsessional neurotic and to the system-formation of some mental patients."[72] "The delusions of paranoiacs have an unpalatable external similarity and internal kinship to the systems of our philosophers."[73]...I do believe that all philosophers would be ideal candidates for psychoanalysis.

Boss: (Puts his note pad back in his pocket.) Yes, well it is good he has been detained at our facility. I fear that he may be suicidal. He tells me his existence is a burden, and he claims that all meaning escapes him.

Freud: "The moment a man questions the meaning and value of life, he is sick, since objectively neither has any existence; by asking this question one is merely admitting to a store of unsatisfied libido to which something else must have happened, a kind of fermentation leading to sadness and depression."[74]

Boss: (Thoughtfully.)...Something traumatic in his childhood must have happened that eventually led to his mental breakdown...

Freud: It goes without saying, "the mental life of the child is important for the psychological understanding of philosophical concepts."[75] "By examining the

---

[70] Keith Hoeller, ed., *Heidegger and Psychology* (Seattle: Review of Existential Psychology and Psychiatry, 1988), 9.

[71] Heidegger, *Zollikon Seminars*, xviii.

[72] Nunburg, *Minutes of the Vienna Psychoanalytic Society*, vol 4, 134.

[73] Freud, *SE* XIII, 73.

[74] Ernest Jones, *The Life and Works of Sigmund Freud*, vol. 3 (New York: Basic Books, 1955), 465.

[75] Nunburg, *Minutes of the Vienna Psychoanalytic Society*, vol 1, 149-50.

primitive psychological situations, which were able to provide the motive for the [philosophical] creations," you will gain "a more penetrating insight" into your patient.[76]

Boss: Yes, of course. I know very little of his childhood history except that he was a physically fragile little boy who dominated his much older peers with his intellect.

Freud: Hmmm…so perhaps his philosophy is a way of compensating for feelings of inferiority and overwhelming guilt[77]…Go further into his history, immerse yourself in his philosophy… "the ability to sublimate, must be traced back to the organic bases."[78] (Shakes head) Philosophers…you do realize that all philosophers are hopelessly insane…each in his own way…(Looking at his pocket-watch.) Oh my, it appears that our session is nearly over.

Boss: (Surprised.) Has it already been an hour?[79]

Freud: (Smiling.) No…But you do realize that this is a dream, don't you? Dreams, as you know, are timeless.

(LIGHTS DIM, BOSS lies back down. FREUD is in darkness now, but BOSS is lit up.)

Boss: (Lying on the couch, his eyes closed, his body back to a "sleeping" position.) If this is a dream, must I still pay you for our session as I did when I was your analysand?[80]

Freud: (In darkness, but audience can hear him chuckling.) Of course you must pay me if you are to get anything significant out of this dream…But I will give you your lunch money, just as I did when you were my analysand and too poor to afford your own meals.

---

[76] Freud, *SE* XIII, 185.

[77] Freud, *SE* XXII, 185.

[78] Freud, *SE* XI, 122-23.

[79] Freud, *SE* XII, 126.

[80] Here, and throughout the play, we often refer to "patients" as "analysands" and "therapists" as "analysts," since this is the proper terminology for psychoanalysis. It is interesting to note that Freud insisted that all patients—including colleagues and family—should pay a significant sum for therapeutic services to encourage patients to work hard, and to insure that therapy was taken seriously. Freud, *SE* XII, 132.

Boss: (Laughing.)

LIGHTS FADE.

END OF ACT I.

ACT II

SCENE 1: Several days have passed. BOSS returns to Heidegger's room. He is carrying his coat and Heidegger's book, *Being and Time*. BOSS pauses at the door, takes a deep breath, and opens the door. HEIDEGGER is lying on his cot, arm over his eyes. Appears to be resting.

Boss: (Hangs his coat on the chair.) Good morning, Professor Heidegger.

Heidegger: (Unresponsive.)

Boss: I've been reading your book…It is quite illuminating. (Puts the book down on the desk, walks back to the chair, scoots it to the cot, and sits down.)

Heidegger: (Puts his hands over his ears and mutters.) Too loud. Too loud.

Boss: (Speaks more softly.) You're hearing the voices, aren't you? Are they loud?

Heidegger: (Turns over on his side, facing away from Boss.) What would you know of voices? You don't *listen*…all this, you say, is in my head…

Boss: No. I've changed my mind. "You are perfectly right. There is no sense in granting one reality priority over another. It would be quite futile for us to maintain that this table before us is more real than your [voices]
merely because they elude my perception and are perceptible only to you. Why don't we let both of them stand as the phenomena they reveal themselves to be? Then there is only one thing worth our attention. That is to consider the full meaning-content of that which discloses itself to us."[81]

Heidegger: (Turns back around. Sits up, somewhat surprised, and looks at Boss, smiles.) I see you are coming to your senses now, Herr Doktor.

Boss: (Now sitting across from Heidegger who sits on the cot.) Yes, well our last therapy session wasn't exactly what I would call, "productive." Afterwards, I began pondering my early days as an analyst…I decided to take Doktor Freud's suggestions…to attempt to understand you better by immersing myself in your world…to try and see the way you see.

---

[81] Boss, *Psychoanalysis and Daseinsanalysis*, 13.

Heidegger: (Shaking head.) Freud![82] Now there's a character worthy of scorn!

Boss: Oh? You've met him?

Heidegger: No, but we did share some mutual acquaintances.

Boss: Oh yes. Doktor Binswanger...we are acquainted as well...and colleagues, of course.

Heidegger: Yes, well Doktor Binswanger and I discussed Freud on occasion. It appears that Freud was not terribly impressed with philosophy, nor did he have the talent...

Boss: Well, Doktor Freud never allowed himself to wander too deeply into the fields of philosophy...He considered it to be too abstract...He thought science was the proper means toward discovering the cure for disturbed mental functioning.

Heidegger: Hmmm...Well, let us not be fooled...regardless of how unreflective science is, it is still rooted in the bits and pieces of philosophical theories...

Boss: Is it now?

Heidegger: Yes, of course...science is merely a piecing together of traditional metaphysics...from Empedocles and Plato to Descartes and Kant....Just because science fails to do it well, doesn't erase the fact that it is grounded in a mishmash of philosophical ideas...

Boss: It is true that Doktor Freud himself mentions a variety of philosophical traditions throughout his writings[83]...Still, he believed that philosophy was predominately speculative, a minor passenger on the way to concrete, scientific discovery...

Heidegger: "[I]t is a great self-deception to believe that the concrete descriptions, separated from 'philosophical' reflection, could be sufficiently enacted. I am very skeptical in this regard. In truth, what is 'philosophical' is

---

[82] In the German/Austrian tradition, one would never address another exclusively by his or her last name, but only by title. Here "Heidegger" neglects to observe the "rules of etiquette" to emphasize his hostility and lack of respect for the man.

[83] Askay and Farquhar, *Apprehending the Inaccessible*, see chapters 1-8.

concrete, and the descriptions are abstract, that is, removed from the ontological meaning which sustains them."[84]

Boss: Hmmm...I'm unclear...What do you mean by "ontological?"

Heidegger: Look, (hits his hand on the bedside table.) "Before we can perceive a table as this or that table, we must receive-perceive that there is something presencing."[85]

Boss: Yes, well it goes without saying that there must be something there first, before we can perceive it...

Heidegger: But that is to make it sound as though there is an object "out there" and we simply stumble upon it.

Boss: Well, isn't that the case? I mean, if it weren't "out there," as you say, we wouldn't stumble in the first place.

Heidegger: (Shaking head.) The way you frame the question...it is already to presuppose an answer that is misleading...As though I am a subject, an entity unto myself...encountering objects outside of me, separate and apart[86]...

Boss: Hmmm...I don't understand...

Heidegger: Actually, you cannot help but understand. That is the point. It is your faculty of understanding that is primary...any "descriptions" or thoughts of a table presuppose understanding...

Boss: So you are saying that in order for that table to exist, I must first have an understanding of "table?"

Heidegger: I am saying that "[t]he phenomenal basis for seeing it at all is provided by the understanding as a disclosive potentiality-for-Being."[87]

Boss: (Tentatively.)...Before we can know a table, we must first understand ourselves...?...

Heidegger: Understand *how it is we understand*[88]...

---

[84] Heidegger, *Zollikon Seminars*, 274.
[85] Ibid., 6.
[86] Heidegger insists that everything hinges upon how one formulates one's questions, and uncritically reflected upon presuppositions are often built into the structure of one's questions. *Zollikon Seminars*, 259; *Being and Time*, 34.
[87] Heidegger, *Being and Time*, 183.

Boss: I see, and science, in your opinion, fails to understand…

Heidegger: Science gives us answers all too quickly, before considering the proper questions "…we must come to the insight that the description of particular phenomena and isolated answers to particular questions are insufficient unless a reflection on the method as such is raised and at the same time kept alive."[89]

Boss: So you reject the scientific method altogether?

Heidegger: No, I do not advocate the complete "abandonment of science." Rather, I am insisting on a reflective relationship to it whereby one thinks through its limitations. It is blind to its methodological presuppositions, and yet proceeds to apply itself to domains inappropriate to it… "Science *is* the new religion" or substitute for philosophy. "Compared to it, any attempt to think of being appears arbitrary and 'mystical.'"[90] The scientist must descend from the throne[91]…

Boss: And you are the one to dethrone the king?

Heidegger: Or perhaps just to reveal his nakedness…

(Both chuckle.)

Boss: (Boss stands up, stretching, picks up his coat from the chair.) Listen, how would you like to depart from this dreary room? Go for a walk? We can discuss your views on science, and stretch our legs.

Heidegger: Hmmm. I don't know. I'm fairly comfortable here…(suspiciously)…Is this part of your therapy?…to remove your patient from the safety of his womb…I mean, *room*?

Boss: (Standing over Heidegger.) You said, "womb"…that's interesting.

Heidegger: I meant to say, "room;" a mere slip of the tongue.

Boss: (Steps back a bit.) So you did…I was just thinking that it has been days since you arrived here. It might be nice to visit the gardens, and to air out your lungs…

---

[88] Ibid., sec. 31.
[89] Heidegger, *Zollikon Seminars*, 94.
[90] Ibid., 18.
[91] Ibid., 50-51.

Heidegger: There are gardens here? (Sits and considers for a moment.) All right then; I suppose it would be good to stretch my legs. (Gets up.)

Boss: (Pointing to Heidegger's umbrella.) You might want to take that, just in case. It isn't raining yet, but this time of year is a bit unpredictable.

Heidegger: Yes, of course. (He walks over to his umbrella, starts putting on his coat.) So how long have you been a psychoanalyst?

Boss: About 22 years now. I did my coursework from 1925 to 1928 and even had the opportunity to be analyzed by the great Doktor Freud while I was a student in Vienna.

Heidegger: (Still putting on his coat, turning to look at Boss.) Ahhhh! So you have been fully indoctrinated by the very reverend Freud himself! (Starts walking toward Boss.)

Boss: (Chuckles.) Yes, I have…Listen you might need your umbrella…It could rain…

Heidegger: Oh, yes, of course. (Walks over to his umbrella, stares at it, as though not seeing it.) I perused that book you gave me the other day.

Boss: Did you? Doktor Freud's, *Papers in Metapsychology*?

Heidegger: Yes…

Boss: And what did you think?

Heidegger: (Walking towards Boss again, without his umbrella.) "[How could] such a highly intelligent and gifted man as Freud produce such artificial, inhuman, indeed absurd and purely fictitious constructions of human beings? [It] literally made me ill…"[92]

Boss: I see. (Both begin to walk out of the room, into the hallway. Both walk slowly together.) So you don't approve of psychoanalysis?

Heidegger: No, I can't say that I do…

Boss: What is it that bothers you specifically?

---

[92] Hoeller, *Heidegger and Psychology*, 9.

Heidegger: Well, the analyst comes into therapy, and, without so much as a modicum of critical reflection, interprets the analysand in terms of his own fundamental philosophical presuppositions.

Boss: Isn't it impossible *not* to do so?

Heidegger: (Stops walking.) Of course it is possible not to do so! Let me ask you, Doktor, are you a thing?

Boss: Excuse me?

Heidegger: Are you a thing? Do I encounter you just as I encounter a table?

Boss: Of course not.

Heidegger: Well then why would you purport to study me just as you study a table?

Boss: I don't consider you a table; Herr Professor...Psychoanalysis acknowledges that humans are different from tables...

Heidegger: How are they different?

Boss: You're teasing me, are you not?

Heidegger: No, I'm quite serious. How are humans different from tables?

Boss: Well, humans are alive.

Heidegger: Yes, and trees are alive as well...

Boss: Yes, but humans have the ability to think, to reason...

Heidegger: And where is that thinking? That reasoning?

Boss: Where is it? Do you mean, where does thinking take place?

Heidegger: No, I mean, how do you get from the material body of the human to the psychical processes of the so-called mind? How do you get from the thought, "I think I will take a walk" to the actual experience of walking? Is it magic?[93]

---

[93] Heidegger, *Zollikon Seminars*, 233.

Boss: (They begin to walk again.) Hmmm…I see where you are going with this…I admit that even Doktor Freud conceded "the leap from the mental to the physical is puzzling."[94]

Heidegger: Of course it is puzzling…(He stops walking) but not because we are puzzled by the fact that we think, experience, live, breathe…We are puzzled because science created the puzzle; science has made it impossible for the pieces to fit together.

Boss: (They begin walking again.) So, if I understand you correctly, you're saying that it is the scientific presuppositions that create the problems?

Heidegger: (Stops walking.) Precisely! Take the unconscious, for example. Psychoanalysis presupposes that there must always be a causal connection, always a reason for why one does what one does. But then they "observe" that there are gaps in one's reasoning, or times when one is not conscious—when one is sleeping, for instance—and so they create an unconscious to account for those gaps…They contrive little black boxes hiding inside the mind[95]…

Boss: (Starts walking.) Hmmm…Yes, that may be true…

Heidegger: But to say that I was aware when I didn't know I was aware…or thinking when I didn't know I was thinking…that is all nonsense!

Boss: (They arrive "outside"—which can simply be the place on the stage where the CURTAINS COME DOWN, and they can walk along the front of the stage.) Yes, I do see a problem with what you are saying…But the unconscious is invaluable to us in psychoanalysis. (Stops and looks up at the "sky.") Hmmm…it's beginning to rain. (Looks at Heidegger for his umbrella and realizes he doesn't have it). You forgot your umbrella.

Heidegger: (Embarrassed laugh.) Yes, it appears that I did.

Boss: Well, in psychoanalysis, leaving behind an umbrella could indicate an unconscious wish to return to the place of departure, where the umbrella was left.

Heidegger: Are you saying that in secret—without my knowledge—I wish to return to my room?

Boss: (Smiling.) Well, do you?

---

[94] Freud, *SE* XVI, 258.
[95] Heidegger, *Zollikon Seminars*, 4; 7-8; 260.

Heidegger: That is absurd!

Boss: Is it? Your room has been a safe shelter these past few days…

Heidegger: Your theories and your explanations are pure contrivance. By way of your hypothesis, you take "the leaving behind of the umbrella" as an isolated fact to be explained and to be ascertained from the outside…I did not leave the umbrella behind—the umbrella is simply not present to me…I can only leave it behind when it is there in the first place[96]…

Boss: …When you say that it is "not present to you" you must mean on some level that you are not conscious of it…But this is what psychoanalysis challenges in the first place, the idea that psychical life equals consciousness.

Heidegger: No…(Shakes his head.)…Look, I too reject such talk, but for different reasons.

Boss: What better alternative is there?

Heidegger: This act of "leaving behind" can be better described phenomenologically. When I leave the umbrella behind, I have no conscious intention…(Looks embarrassed for a moment.) But let's take a different example.

Boss: You don't feel comfortable talking about your own reasons for leaving your umbrella behind?

Heidegger: It isn't that at all. I just believe that my point will be made much clearer if I use another example.

Boss: But I would prefer to discuss why you left your umbrella behind after I had twice reminded you to take it.

Heidegger: (Unhappy with Boss. Starts to turn back.) Perhaps we should go back to my room! You obviously aren't interested in what I have to say…

Boss: No, that's not true. I apologize. Please continue with your own example…

Heidegger: (Turns back to Boss again. Says sternly.) Are you sure? Do you think that for a few moments, you can listen to me and really hear what I am about to tell you?

---

[96] Ibid., 214-15.

Boss: Yes, of course. Please continue.

Heidegger: All right…Let's say a woman goes to her lover and she leaves her purse in his apartment when she departs. Since, the man whom the woman visited is not indifferent to her, her departure is such that by leaving she is still present there more than ever. The purse is not present to her at all because she is so totally with the man while she departs. In this kind of departure the purse is left behind because the woman was so much with her friend already during her visit in the room that the purse was not present to her even at that time. Here the "going somewhere" simply does not exist for her. If the same woman were to depart from someone to whom she was indifferent in order to go to the city, then she would not forget her purse. Rather she would take it with her because it is essential. For the woman this then would be the relationship in which she would be involved. Here it is only the departure to the city that matters. This having-been with this other person to whom she is indifferent now is finished.[97]

Boss: From a psychoanalytical point of view, this situation is far too simple in terms of how repression and the unconscious operate…Also, haven't you begged the question by assuming that the woman would not forget her purse if this one reason did not hold? But this neglects the complex processes of the unconscious….

Heidegger: "When I leave the umbrella behind I don't think of taking it with me. When I forget something painful I don't want to think about it. Here, *it* does not slip away from me, but *I* let it slip away from me. This letting something slip away from me happens in such a way that I occupy myself more and more with something else so that what is uncomfortable may slip away."[98] The very painfulness itself is indeed already an indication of the fact that I was…(pauses)…I mean, it is indicative that SHE was—the woman with the purse—and still is afflicted by the painful event of youth. But she does not want to deal with it, with that which is painful. It is an evasion from herself as a self that is continuously afflicted by the painful.

Boss: Interesting that you started to talk about yourself for a bit, then switched back to talking about our hypothetical purse woman…Are there painful events that you "let slip away?"

Heidegger: (Frustrated.)…We are talking about the unconscious and how it is rooted in a misconception of what it means to be human…Seriously, if you are going to be difficult, we might as well go back to my room.

---

[97] Ibid., 168-70.
[98] Ibid., 169.

Boss: No, no...please continue.

Heidegger: All I was going to say is that "[i]n her avoidance of herself, she is present to herself in an unthematic way, and the more she engages in this avoidance, the less she knows about the avoidance. Rather, she is entirely absorbed in this avoidance in a non-reflective way."[99]

Boss: I see...and that is why the notion of an unconscious is unnecessary?

Heidegger: Yes, precisely!

Boss: Hmmmm...Well, I have to say that our friend Doktor Freud would point out your non sequitur that "she is also aware of this painful event, otherwise it could not be painful."[100] "To begin with it may happen that an affect or emotion is perceived, but misconstrued. By the repression of its proper presentation it is forced to become connected with another idea, and is now interpreted by consciousness as the expression of this other idea. If we restore the true connection, we call the original affect "unconscious," although the affect was never unconscious but its ideational presentation had undergone repression."[101] In other words, she might not know the content of the painful event as an idea, and yet still feel its pain.

Heidegger: Unconscious pain? (Shaking his head.) No, that makes no sense.

Boss: All right, then. Let's take another example. How does your philosophy account for dreams?

Heidegger: Dreams?

Boss: Yes, dreams. According to Doktor Freud, dreams are the royal road to the unconscious.[102]

Heidegger: (Shaking his head.) "The dream world cannot be separated as an object domain unto itself, but rather the dream world belongs in a certain way to the continuity of being-in-the-world. It is likewise a being-in-the-world."[103]

---

[99] Ibid., 170.
[100] Askay and Farquhar, *Apprehending the Inaccessible*, 227.
[101] Freud, *SE* XIV, 177-78.
[102] What Freud actually wrote was, "The interpretation of dreams is the royal road to a knowledge of the unconscious activities of the mind." (*SE* V, 608.) Note that Freud's way of stating the importance of dreams does not necessarily presuppose the creation of little black boxes in the mind as Heidegger and Boss concluded and criticized. Freud was not interested in objectifying the unconscious processes nor specifying a special locality.
[103] Heidegger, *Zollikon Seminars*, 229.

Boss: Doktor Freud believed that dreams contain hidden meanings, and that by studying a dream, one could reveal a great deal about a person's unconscious motivations.

Heidegger: (Chuckling.) Seriously! How absurd! (Shakes his head.) Well, I should tell you, Doktor, that I have had only one recurring dream in my entire life. I dream it often and it is always the same.[104]

Boss: (Very curious.) That *is* interesting! What is your dream?

Heidegger: I am attempting to take my matriculation examination, and the high school teachers, who sit before me, harass me with their "relentless questions."[105] (Shakes head and looks down.)

Boss: (A bit disappointed.) Oh? (Pauses while he stares at Heidegger for a moment.)

Heidegger: (Looks up at Boss.) My God, here I am a world-renowned philosopher and *they* are harassing me!

Boss: (Confused.) Hmmmm, I see. (Pause.) And that is all?

Heidegger: (Slightly offended.) Well...Yes. (Pause.) Sorry to disappoint you...

Boss: (Apologetic.) Oh, no, no, no. That's quite all right. I just assumed your dream would be more elaborate.

Heidegger: (Shrugs.) Well, it is a *frequently* recurring dream. Surely that is of importance.

Boss: Yes, of course.

Heidegger: And I assume that "stereotypical dreams recur only as long as the problem in them is not resolved and is not completely worked out in the waking state."[106]

Boss: Yes, that is true.

---

[104] Ibid., 229; 245; 340.
[105] Hoeller, *Heidegger and Psychology*, 13; see also Heidegger, *Zollikon Seminars*, 229.
[106] Heidegger, *Zollikon Seminars*, 229.

Heidegger: (Curious.) So what hidden secrets do you suppose it reveals, Herr Doktor?

Boss: (Thinking a moment.) Hmmmm...I'm not certain, but I assume it indicates some constriction in your worldview[107]

Heidegger: (A bit disappointed.) Oh, I see. (Pause.) Well, what would Doktor Freud say about my dream?

Boss: I imagine he would consider it an indication that you have "done something wrong or failed to do something properly...[you] expect to be punished...[and you] feel the burden of responsibility."[108]

Heidegger: (Angry and defensive.) That is utterly ridiculous. "Dreams are not symptoms and consequences of something lying hidden behind [them], but they themselves are what they show and *only* this."[109] (Shakes head.)...Your Freud was convoluted in his thinking...He was nothing more than a misguided Kantian/Schopenhauerian in disguise[110]...Not a particularly clever disguise, I might add...

Boss: Be that as it may, I find it interesting that you so vehemently reject Doktor Freud, when much of what he says is quite pertinent to your own situation...

Heidegger: (Defensively.) My own situation?

Boss: (Gently.) You are here in this sanatorium for a reason, my good professor. In every example you have presented, you reveal your own agony...And you lash out at Doktor Freud as though he is the sole creator of your misery...

Heidegger: (With sadness, looking down.) Yes, well Doktor Freud made countless mistakes, as we have seen...

Boss: Yes, I suppose he did. (Pause. Gently.) And you have made mistakes too, have you not? (Looks directly at Heidegger who is still looking down.)

---

[107] Ibid., 13; see also Medard Boss, *Existential Foundations of Medicine and Psychology,* trans. Steven Conway and Anne Cleaves (New York: Aronson, 1979), 168-69.

[108] Freud, *SE* IV, 274.

[109] Heidegger, *Zollikon Seminars*, 245. This is an example, from a Freudian viewpoint, of Heidegger concealing the true motive for holding this position.

[110] Heidegger, *Zollikon Seminars*, 207. Heidegger did not actually recognize the Schopenhauerian influences in Freud's work, but this is an important point to be made in the context of this play.

Listen; do you suppose it is possible that you have a great many painful memories that you have let slip away from you…and that your hostility towards science and psychoanalysis is, in part, a way of evading yourself?

Heidegger: (Annoyed and stronger now. Looks directly at Boss.) The problem I have with psychoanalysis is that the analysts wind up imposing their own uncritically held interpretive frameworks upon their patients! This is to unduly intervene in their lives, and to, in effect, make their choices for them…

Boss: (Confused.) I'm not trying to make choices for you…

Heidegger: I'm not talking about you personally…I'm just saying that a far better alternative to psychoanalysis is to let the patients *presence themselves* in terms of their own self-understanding, explore their possibilities with them, and most importantly not try to impose anything upon them by way of theoretical insights. This would be to engage in what I call "anticipatory care"…After all, the goal is to enable the patient to become an authentic person in his own right, is it not?[111]

Boss: Well certainly the goal is to help the patient discover what is blocking him or her from being a whole person[112]…

Heidegger: But to accomplish that goal, you must first know what it means to be a whole person, am I right?

Boss: Yes, of course.

Heidegger: And you do this through a process of questions and answers…Correct?

Boss: Well, not entirely, but please go on…

Heidegger: The questions you ask, those therapeutic questions…you must be very careful about the way in which you raise the questions…It is crucial to structure your questions so that they are as appropriate for the therapeutic task as possible.[113]

Boss: …That makes sense…

---

[111] Ibid., 309-12.

[112] Boss, *Psychoanalysis and Daseinsanalysis*, 195; 201.

[113] Heidegger, *Zollikon Seminars*, 33; 37; 259.

Heidegger: "The art of interpretation is the art of asking the right questions."[114] If one fails to understand this, therapy is adrift.

Boss: Yes, of course…

Heidegger: Do you recall our first meeting? You asked me, "What are you anxious about?" and I replied, "nothing."

Boss: Yes, I assumed you were in denial and not ready to discuss your situation with me.

Heidegger: Exactly! And there is your problem! The very way in which you structured your question presupposed that my anxiety must be about "something."[115] The result was that your question—posed as it was—precluded any real understanding of what I was experiencing.

Boss: So you weren't intentionally trying to evade my question? (Shakes head, looking down.) Interesting. (Looks at Heidegger.) So what did you mean when you said, "nothing?"

Heidegger: I was experiencing that profound aspect of the human condition that I call "the nothing." That which makes possible all that we are, and yet discloses the lack of foundation of our existence. It was precisely my anxiety that disclosed "the nothing."[116]

Boss: (Embarrassed and yet, reflective.) Oh, I see. And I cut you off from that, didn't I? I imposed my own interpretative framework over you instead of just "letting you be" in terms of your own experiencing…

Heidegger: Precisely! "As a[n] [analyst] you must, as it were, stand back and let the other human being be."[117] Stand back, and let me be!

Boss: (Shakes head in agreement…thoughtfully.) Yes, I understand…I deeply apologize for our first session. It was not one of my best moments as an analyst.

(Loud thunder…it begins to rain heavily)

---

[114] Ibid., 54; 96.
[115] Heidegger points out that in the everyday world we often conflate 'angst' with 'fear,' and the result is catastrophic for the patient. Heidegger, *Being and Time*, 230.
[116] Heidegger, *Basic Writings*, 103.
[117] Heidegger, *Zollikon Seminars*, 211.

Boss: Oh my! (Both look up to the sky.) It seems the gods have heard you as well...(Laughter.)   We best be getting back inside...I believe that your wisdom is enough of a lightning bolt for me today...I'd rather not suffer through an actual execution...I mean electrocution, in this angry thunderstorm!

LIGHTS FADE.

END OF SCENE.

ACT II

SCENE 2: After sojourning[118] with Heidegger, BOSS returns to his office. FREUD is sitting in a chair by the couch, going over some lecture notes. BOSS sees him and walks to the couch, and sits down across from him.[119]

Boss: (To Freud:) I thought you might be here. (Chuckles.)

Freud: (Looking up from his papers.) You find me humorous today?

Boss: Oh, not at all...It's just that...well, you *are* dead, and yet you are here...and it doesn't even bother me whether you are real or not.[120]

Freud: (Looking contemplative.) Hmmm...No, that shouldn't bother you too much. (Chuckles.) We both know that I am your unconscious wish...

Boss: (More serious now.) Are you? (Shaking head.) I'm not so certain anymore.

Freud: (Confused.) Not certain? Not certain of what? Not certain of the unconscious?

Boss: Well...of course there is an unconscious...or maybe not. Professor Heidegger says that to create an unconscious is to invent little black boxes...

Freud: Oh, come now, dear friend, you can't be serious. After all our research, all those years of work...of battling both science and philosophy in hopes of making true progress...and you are back to questioning the very foundation of psychoanalysis?

Boss: No, of course not. It's just that this patient of mine has shown me an alternative way of looking at human existence. His philosophy potentially offers new insights...

---

[118] Heidegger makes a point of using the term "sojourning in the clearing." Sojourning is dwelling in one's comportment in the world. Heidegger, *Zollikon Seminars*, 144.

[119] Sitting across from Freud (as opposed to being reclined on the couch in a therapeutic context) is symbolic that this conversation will be more in line with an "adversarial" confrontation, according to Freud's psychoanalytic recommendations. See Freud, *SE* XII, 133ff.

[120] This shows a movement in Boss' thinking, from a more scientific/Freudian concern as to whether or not "hallucinations" are real, to a more phenomenological perspective of meaning.

Freud: (Frustrated with arms folded.) "We have nothing to expect from philosophy except that it will once again haughtily point out to us the intellectual inferiority of the object of our study."[121]

Boss: (Stands up and paces a bit.) No, no…it's not like that…Professor Heidegger's hermeneutic phenomenological ontology[122] may provide a better grounding for psychoanalytic therapy…one that is more appropriate than the scientific Weltanschauung.[123]

Freud: Have you gone *mad*? Psychoanalysis "is quite unfit to construct a Weltanschauung of its own: it must accept the scientific one."[124] "Our best hope for the future is that intellect—the scientific spirit, reason—may in process of time establish a dictatorship in the mental life of man."[125]

Boss: (Looking confused and says somewhat timidly.)…Hmmm…didn't you yourself emphasize that it is unacceptable for psychoanalysis to "place itself in the service of a particular philosophical outlook on the world and should urge this upon the patient to ennoble him [and that]…this is after-all only tyranny[?]"[126] Aren't you urging a particular philosophical outlook on your colleagues and patients by so strongly advocating the scientific Weltanschauung?

Freud: You misunderstood my intention…

Boss: At any rate, Professor Heidegger would argue that your position is to already presuppose certain philosophical commitments…

Freud: Of course it is, but that poses no problems… "…[S]ince the intellect and the mind are objects for scientific research in exactly the same way as any non-human things, [p]sychoanalysis has a special right to speak for the scientific Weltanschauung at this point, since it cannot be reproached with having neglected what is mental in the picture of the universe. Its contribution to science lies precisely in having extended research to the mental field."[127]

Boss: But doesn't philosophy have some role in this?

---

[121] Freud, *SE* XV, 97-98.
[122] Askay and Farquhar, *Apprehending the Inaccessible*, 414.
[123] "Weltanschauung" is the German word for "an intellectual construction" which generates a particular "worldview." Freud, *SE* XXII, 158.
[124] Freud, *SE* XXII, 158.
[125] Ibid., 171.
[126] Freud, *SE* XVII, 165-66.
[127] Freud, *SE* XXII, 159.

Freud: "Philosophy is not opposed to science, it behaves like a science and works in part by the same methods; it departs from it, however, by clinging to the illusion of being able to present a picture of the universe which is without gaps and is coherent, though one which is bound to collapse with every fresh advance in our knowledge. It goes astray in its method by over-estimating the epistemological value of our logical operations and by accepting other sources of knowledge such as intuition."[128]

Boss: Well, Professor Heidegger would agree that such "calculative" modes of thinking[129] have been egregiously predominant and exclusionary of other ways of thinking in Western cultures.

Freud: But you said he rejects the unconscious…or as you put it, the creation of little black boxes…

Boss: Yes, well…Professor Heidegger would say that psychoanalysis is still operating within the epistemological paradigm of traditional metaphysics, that you have attempted to meld together the philosophies of Galileo, Newton, Descartes, Kant, Nietzsche…

Freud: (Interrupting defensively.) Wait a minute! "…Nietzsche's ideas have had no influence whatsoever on my own work."[130] I intentionally did not read Nietzsche[131]…

Boss: (Sits down across from Freud) Yes, well…(Nervously clearing his throat.) But you did utilize a great deal of philosophical ideas in the development of your metapsychology.

Freud: Well, of course! My metapsychological theory was "…designed to clarify and subject to a more profound study the theoretical assumptions upon which a psychoanalytic system could be based."[132] This is why my metapsychology represented to me the furthest goal psychology could attain, "the consummation of psycho-analytic research."[133] Indeed, I saw it as the ground of psychoanalysis that in turn ultimately grounded *philosophy* itself.

---

[128] Ibid., 160-61.

[129] In his *Discourse on Thinking*, Heidegger insists this mode of thinking is solely able to direct itself to objects or things (p. 46).

[130] Nunburg, *Minutes of the Vienna Psychoanalytic Society*, vol. 1, 359-60.

[131] Freud claimed never to have read Nietzsche (*SE* XIV, 15-16) "because it was plain that [he] would find insights in Nietzsche very similar to psycho-analytic ones." (*SE* XX, 60). Apparently, Freud did not want to contaminate his theory prior to scientific observation. For a more extensive discussion on this topic see Askay and Farquhar, *Apprehending the Inaccessible*, 90-93.

[132] Freud, *SE* XIV, 222n.

[133] Ibid., 181.

Boss: Yes, and you used philosophical ideas…

Freud: (Interjecting.)…In accordance with scientific procedure…

Boss: Yes, of course…in accordance with scientific procedure…to ground psychoanalysis.

Freud: Yes. So?

Boss: So, your metapsychological theory is grounded in traditional philosophical theory.

Freud: In accordance with scientific procedure…

Boss: Yes. (Both stare at one another. Pause.)

Freud: And your point is?

Boss: Well, my point is that maybe…at times…you have overlooked the impact philosophy has had on the development of psychoanalysis…

Freud: (Gets up to pour himself a drink—alcohol.) I told you that I have little capacity for philosophy…

Boss: (Still sitting.) Yes, but you also admitted to employing philosophical ideas…you said that Schopenhauer was the foremost philosophical forerunner of psychoanalysis.[134]

Freud: (A   little   frustrated…Pouring   drink.   Muttering.) Schopenhauer…Schopenhauer…Schopenhauer…(Pause.   Takes a sip of his drink.)   "The large extent to which psychoanalysis coincides with the philosophy of Schopenhauer…is not to be traced to my acquaintance with his teaching. I read Schopenhauer very late in my life…"[135]

Boss: I see…well there is the question of priority…

Freud: "I was less concerned with the question of priority than with keeping my mind unembarrassed."[136]

Boss: Unembarrassed?

---

[134] Freud, *SE* VII, 143-44.
[135] Freud, *SE* XX, 59.
[136] Ibid., 60.

Freud: (Turns toward Boss.) Look, it just so happens that early on in my development of psychoanalysis, I "simply unwittingly steered [my] course into the harbors of Schopenhauer's philosophy."[137]

Boss: (A bit nervous.) Yes…

Freud: (Defensively.) Well, "…why should not a bold thinker have guessed something that is afterwards confirmed by sober and painstaking detailed research? Moreover, there is nothing that has not been said already, and similar things had been said by many people before Schopenhauer…"[138]

Boss: (Shrugging.)

Freud: (Walks over to Boss, stands over him, voice raised.) So what?

Boss: (Quietly.) Nothing…That's all…

Freud: (Angry.) No it's NOT all…I can see it in your face! What are you implying?

Boss: (Quietly.) Well…I was just wondering…

Freud: (Still angry.) Wondering what? Speak up! I can't hear you!

Boss: (Nervously clears throat and speaks up a bit.) Did you simply forget the impact Schopenhauer had on your development of psychoanalysis?

Freud: (Suspiciously.) You know that "…it is [my] belief that no one forgets anything without some secret reason or hidden motive…"[139]

Boss: (Nervously.) I know…

Freud: (Again, a bit angry.) Well what?

Boss: It's just that so much of psychoanalysis can be directly traced to Schopenhauer's philosophy…

Freud: (Loudly.) Well, hell! If you are going to trace everything to its original roots… "Careful psychological investigation…reveals hidden and long-forgotten sources which gave the stimulus to the apparently original

---

[137] Freud, *SE* XVIII, 49-50.

[138] Freud, *SE* XXII, 107.

[139] Freud, *SE* IX, 22.

ideas, and it replaces the ostensible new creation by a revival of something forgotten applied to fresh material. There is nothing to regret in this; we had no right to expect that what was 'original' could be untraceable and undetermined."[140]

Boss: (Still nervous.) It's just that you claimed that your theory of repression was original...

Freud: (Insisting.) It was original!!

Boss: And yet Schopenhauer—even according to you—had an awareness of the mechanisms of repression...

Freud: (Boiling now.) So? So what? My theory of repression was original![141]

Boss: ...Is it possible that *you repressed the origins of your theory of repression according to your own theory*?

Freud: (Throws hands up in air, spilling his drink.) Now, THAT is utterly absurd! (Calming a bit and wiping the drink off his suit.) It is true that Schopenhauer may have guessed correctly...it appears that he may have been aware of the mechanism of repression...but all he accomplished was strictly within the realm of philosophy...(Shaking head.) This is precisely why we must remain within the scientific realm and not stray too far in our speculations...

Boss: Yes, but Professor Heidegger's point is that science itself is grounded in philosophy...

Freud: Well hell! If you put it that way, every thought, every idea is grounded in philosophy!

Boss: Precisely!

Freud: (Looks at Boss with contempt.)

Boss: And because all ideas are philosophical in nature, we must be aware of our presuppositions.

---

[140] Freud, *SE* XIX, 261.
[141] Freud, *SE* XIV, 15.

Freud: (Sarcastically. Standing over Boss.) Oh, "[l]et us humbly accept the contempt with which [philosophers] look down on us from the vantage-ground of their superior needs."[142]

Boss: (Stands up to face Freud.) Well, Professor Heidegger's point is that if we acknowledge the philosophical presuppositions grounding our scientific theories, we can see where we've gone astray…find an alternative philosophy that would more appropriately consider questions regarding what it means to be as a human being…We have lost track of our wonderment and understanding of Being…

Freud: (Scowling, in a condescending tone.) "We know well enough how little light science has so far been able to throw on the problems that surround us. But however much ado the philosophers may make cannot alter the situation…such a benighted traveler may sing aloud in the dark to deny his own fears but for all that he will not see an inch further beyond his nose."[143]

LIGHTS DIM

END OF ACT II

[INTERMISSION]

---

[142] Freud, *SE* XX, 96.
[143] Ibid.

ACT III

SCENE 1: BOSS enters Heidegger's room. HEIDEGGER is sitting at his desk. He appears to be scribbling furiously on a piece of paper.[144] BOSS walks over to his desk.

Boss: My you are working hard today…

(Heidegger does not respond.)

Boss: (Looking over Heidegger's shoulder at the piece of paper, he sees that Heidegger is drawing faces on it). Extraordinary!

Heidegger: "They come…out of nowhere, just suddenly appear, emerge from somewhere behind the drawing paper, and all of a sudden they are there, looking at me…"[145]

Boss: These faces! They look frightening! Judgmental…

Heidegger: Yes! They want to control me, to control everyone…

Boss: Hmmm…Interesting…

Heidegger: (Still drawing.) "Sometimes there is no contour of a head delimiting [their] features from the surrounding universe, or perhaps from the nothingness from which they come."[146]

Boss: They come from the "nothing"…?

Heidegger: "From the nothing all beings *as* beings come to be."[147]

Boss: Yes, the nothing…

Heidegger: "The Nothing directs us toward the beings that are slipping away as a whole…the nothing discloses these beings in their concealed alien quality as that which is radically other."[148]

---

[144] In *Psychoanalysis and Daseinsanalysis*, Boss utilizes his patient's drawings to better immerse himself in the patient's immediate experience, and gain more penetrating psychological insights.
[145] Boss, *Psychoanalysis and Daseinsanalysis*, 11.
[146] Ibid.
[147] Heidegger, *Basic Writings*, 110.
[148] *Ibid.* 104-5.

Boss: Who is the other?

Heidegger: "Everyone is the other and no one is himself."[149]

Boss: Where are *you* in this picture? (Pointing to the picture.) Is this you, the one standing in the open space?

Heidegger: No, no! "The more openly the 'they' behaves, the harder it is to grasp, and the slier it is, but the less is it nothing at all."[150]

Boss: I see, so this person is "hard to grasp"...

Heidegger: Hard to grasp...

Boss: Their mouths are open, what do they say?

Heidegger: "We [must] take pleasure and enjoy ourselves [only] as *they* take pleasure; we read, see, and judge...as *they* see and judge...we find 'shocking' what *they* find shocking."[151]

Boss: Is there no place for you to have your privacy...your private thoughts, perhaps?

Heidegger: No! ...They "control every way in which the world...gets interpreted...and [they are] always right..."[152]

Boss: Is there no space where you can be right?

Heidegger: (Scoots back in his chair a bit.) No...no space...

Boss: (Looking at Heidegger.) Your body is shaking...

Heidegger: (Closes his eyes.) ...There is something queer about it...It "is not yet within striking distance, but it is coming close."[153]

Boss: (Gets the other chair and brings it to where Heidegger is sitting. Sits down next to Heidegger.) What's coming close?

---

[149] Heidegger, *Being and Time*, 165.
[150] Ibid., 166.
[151] Ibid., 164.
[152] Ibid., 165.
[153] Ibid., 179-80.

Heidegger: (Eyes still closed.)   I don't know…something…something is threatening me…(Starts to tremble.)

Boss: (Softly.) Don't be afraid…I'm here with you…

Heidegger: (Snapping out of it.) Afraid? (Pulls away.) No, I am not afraid…I do not fear…Fear is always fear of something… "Fear is anxiety, fallen into the 'world,' inauthentic, and as such, hidden from itself."[154] This is different…

Boss: Oh? How is it different?

Heidegger: This is anxiety… "That in the face of which one has anxiety is not an entity within-the-world…[it] is completely indefinite…anxiety is characterized by the fact that what threatens is *nowhere*.   Anxiety 'does not know' what that in the face of which it is anxious… 'Nowhere,' however, does not signify nothing: this is where any region lies, and there too lies any disclosedness of the world…"[155]

Boss: Hmmm…I see…

Heidegger: (Sitting up straight.) "Therefore that which threatens cannot bring itself close from a definite direction within what is close by; it is already 'there,' and yet nowhere; it is so close that it is oppressive and stifles one's breath, and yet it is nowhere."[156]

Boss: Hmmm…You just seemed so frightened a moment ago.   But I see now that you do not fear, as you say…

Heidegger: No, I do not fear…You must not mistake angst for fear…everything will be thrown into confusion.[157]

Boss: (Clearing his throat.) Yes, of course…

Heidegger: "Dasein's falling into the 'they'…is…'fleeing' in the face of itself.   But one is not necessarily fleeing whenever one shrinks back in the face of something or turns away from it."[158]

Boss: I see…

---

[154] Ibid., 234.
[155] Ibid., 231.
[156] Ibid.
[157] Heidegger, *History of the Concept of Time*, 289.
[158] Heidegger, *Being and Time*, 230.

Heidegger: *"The turning-away of falling is grounded rather in anxiety, which in turn is what first makes fear possible."*[159]

Boss: So you weren't experiencing fear…

Heidegger: No.

Boss: (Stands up and looks at Heidegger's drawing again.) Hmmmm…That's interesting…

Heidegger: (Looking.) What?

Boss: Look here! (Points to picture.)…Among all these nasty faces…I see a woman…beautiful, mysterious…hidden…

Heidegger: (Looking closely at the picture.) A woman?

Boss: Yes, see this young woman…almost a girl…

Heidegger: No, there is no young woman…that's just a shadow[160]

Boss: No, look! You can see her. She's subtle, but distinct, there in the background…

Heidegger: (Turns away abruptly.) It was wrong of me to look at her.

Boss: No, it's OK…Look, she has a veil[161]…you can't see her clearly…

Heidegger: (Distressed, unwilling to look at the picture.) "[Her] fearsomeness remains veiled"[162]

---

[159] Ibid.

[160] Hannah Arendt wrote "The Shadows"—early self-reflections—and gave a copy to Heidegger as a gift in April 1925. Hannah Arendt, and Martin Heidegger, *Letters 1925-1975*, ed. Ursula Ludz, trans. Andrew Shields (New York: Harcourt, 2004), 12-16; 222n1.

[161] "Veiled" is an interesting metaphor from both Hannah Arendt's and Martin Heidegger's life/work. Ettinger wrote, "It is reported that as a young teenager Hannah was fascinated by family tales about a beautiful vanished aunt who…knew her stunning face only from behind a thick veil." Elzbieta Ettinger, *Hannah Arendt/Martin Heidegger* (New Haven: Yale University Press, 1995), 18. Heidegger also makes numerous references throughout his works to the "veiled," especially in reference to the "concealed."

[162] Heidegger, *Being and Time*, 180.

Boss: (Sits back in his chair.) Do you recognize her?

Heidegger: (Looking sad.) "...it is the *same* gaze that leaped toward me on the lectern..."[163] ...Her eyes, so deep and dark[164]...

Boss: Who is she?

Heidegger: (Eyes closed.) She was so shy,[165] so perfect...She knew I was lonely, and she came to my office[166]...I wanted to protect her, to possess her...

Boss: What is her name?

Heidegger: (Eyes wide open.) No! We cannot discuss her...I feel such shame, such disgust...

Boss: (Gently.)...If I am to help you, you must be open...

Heidegger: (Stiff body language.) I cannot tell you...she is my secret...She took pleasure in being my secret[167]...She knew very well what she was doing...

Boss: What was she doing?

Heidegger: Her adoration...she knew...

Boss: What did she know?

Heidegger: Too much! Everything! It was all so wrong. (Looks at Boss.) "Why is love rich beyond all other possible human experiences and a sweet burden to those seized in its grasp?"[168]

Boss: You loved her...

---

[163] Arendt, *Letters 1925-1975*, 222n 4.

[164] Ibid., 44. Ettinger also speculates that Heidegger was first attracted to Arendt's "large, dark eyes." *Hannah Arendt/Martin Heidegger*, 15.

[165] Arendt, *Letters 1925-1975*, 17.

[166] After having watched her for some time, Heidegger asked Hannah Arendt to come to his office for a "conference." Arendt was a first year student, 18 years old, and Heidegger was her professor, age 35 (Ettinger, *Hannah Arendt/Martin Heidegger*, 10-16; see also Arendt, *Letters: 1925-1975*, 3).

[167] Arendt, *Letters 1925-1975*, 18-19. Ettinger speculates that Arendt was attracted to the secrecy of their meetings "for the aura of mystery was as alluring to her as it was to him." (*Hannah Arendt/Martin Heidegger*, 18).

[168] Arendt, *Letters 1925-1975*, 4.

Heidegger: "Everything should be simple and clear and pure…"[169]   But she lied…(Shaking head, looking down.) It was meant to be pure, but through her, the "demonic struck me."[170]   I could not keep my "instincts under control"[171]…such a "storm." "…[O]ur storm…"[172]

Boss: She was your lover?

Heidegger: (Looking down.) She told me it was spiritual…we could create our own spirituality[173]…We could be above it all…We could laugh at *them*! (Raising head and smiling.) My dear Hannah, such delicate strength…

Boss: Hannah Arendt? Was she your lover?

Heidegger: My salvation…my hope, my soul…(Shuddering.) Oh, I feel so dirty.

Boss: What is dirty about loving a beautiful woman?

Heidegger: "…[E]verything turns back into ruthlessness and violence…"[174] But it was her choice to leave…I didn't stop her…It was best for her[175]…

Boss: What happened to her?

Heidegger: (Shaking his head.) If what they said was true, how could I have loved her?[176] *"No one* took such risks as I did."[177]

Boss: What risks? I don't understand…

Heidegger: I feel such disgust…such shame…we mustn't discuss her…They will hear…

---

[169] Ibid., 3.

[170] Ibid., 6.

[171] Ibid., 17.

[172] Ibid., 9.

[173] Ibid., 20-26.

[174] Ibid., 41.

[175] It appears that Heidegger encouraged Arendt to leave Marburg where they were professor/student. Heidegger wrote a letter to Arendt contending that it was for her own good, but Ettinger speculates that it was more likely for Heidegger's good (*Hannah Arendt/Martin Heidegger*, 21-22).

[176] Arendt, *Letters 1925-1975*, 52-53.

[177] Heidegger wrote to Jaspers on April 8, 1950. In this letter, he minimized his Nazi involvement by pointing out how much he had done to help the Jewish students. Beimel, Walter and Hans Saner, eds., *Martin Heidegger/Karl Jaspers Briefwechsel 1920-1963* (Frankfurt am Main; Klostermann; Munich: Piper, 1990), 202.

Boss: Who will hear?

Heidegger: Yes, who will hear…(Crouching down in his chair.) The spies[178]…they are watching me…waiting…They are in my home…I can no longer be at home in myself…

Boss: You say they are spying? "…[S]pying occurs only as a form of preparation for war…"[179]

Heidegger: Yes, they are preparing for war…I am the enemy…I tried to show them…I didn't know…I was innocent…deceived…used…

Boss: "…[War] occurs only where two enemies exist, mutually barred against each other and consequently antagonistic to one another, and where one party wants to annihilate the other or at least to conquer it and bring it under its own dominion…"[180]

Heidegger: Yes, there is so much warring…so much noise…(Covers ears.) I can't stand the pressure in my ears any longer[181]…

(Silence for a moment.)

Boss: It's OK, honestly…You are safe now…no one can harm you…(Pause.) "How would it be if you were to allow everything there is a right to be, and to hold yourself open to all that wants to come to you…"[182]

Heidegger: (Uncups ears to some degree and looks at Boss.)

---

[178] It should be noted that references to "spies" are found in both Boss' description of his patient's drawings (Boss, *Psychoanalysis and Daseinsanalysis*, 10) and in Heidegger's statement during the Verification Commission (Ettinger, *Hannah Arendt/Martin Heidegger*, 63). Heidegger was under surveillance by the Nazi party, and he was clearly uncomfortable with the "spies." Safranski, *Martin Heidegger*, 318-31; Ott, *Martin Heidegger,* 254f. Heidegger also felt he was being watched closely by officials of the Catholic Church given his debt to them for his education and other subsequent considerations.
[179] Boss, *Psychoanalysis and Daseinsanalysis*, 13.
[180] Ibid.
[181] This is also in reference to Boss' patient's description in *Psychoanalysis and Daseinsanalysis* where he writes that "…every single sound had taken on an uncanny meaning…" (p. 6).
[182] Boss, *Psychoanalysis and Daseinsanalysis*, 13.

Boss: "Why not try giving up all this fighting and defending of yourself? Let the spies come and give them full power to do as they wish, and just see what happens."[183]

Heidegger: (Quizzically.) Let the spies come?

Boss: Yes, let yourself just be, let them come…do not fight…

Heidegger: (Lets out a deep breath, hands drop from his ears.) I'm so tired of fighting…I cannot fight them any longer…"Everything gained by a struggle becomes just something to be manipulated. Every secret loses its force."[184]

Boss: You don't have to fight them anymore…Just let them come…We will deal with them together…

Heidegger: You must help me, Doktor…Help me clear away these "concealments and obscurities"…help me break up of the disguises with which I bar my own way[185]…

Boss: Yes, of course! I am here for you…Everything is going to be all right…

LIGHTS FADE

END OF SCENE

---

[183] Ibid., 13-14.

[184] Heidegger, *Being and Time*, 165.

[185] Ibid., 167.

ACT III

SCENE 2: BOSS returns to his office after his session with Heidegger. In his office, FREUD is sitting in the chair by the couch, reading. FREUD has a cigar in his pocket. BOSS has his briefcase in hand—containing a photo of Heidegger and Boss. BOSS sets the briefcase down, beside his desk, and walks over to the couch.

Boss: I'm so glad you are still here.

Freud: (Looking up from his book.) Yes, well it is interesting that I continue to be in your thoughts. Have you not found some resolution to make my presence unnecessary?

Boss: (Sits down across from him.   Excited.)   I had my first major breakthrough with my analysand today.

Freud: Congratulations!

Boss: (Excited.) Yes! I did as we discussed and immersed myself in his philosophy to see how it could reveal the roots of his agony.

Freud: Very good! And what did you find?

Boss: His philosophy offers us the key to his way of looking at the world.

Freud: Of course it does!   Were you able to uncover the psychological mechanisms that have brought about his breakdown?

Boss: No, actually I discovered that I had to remain within the immediate experience…

Freud: Oh? And what did you find?

Boss: To be honest, I did not encounter the "slightest evidence which would give us the right to assume the actual presence of primary, instinctual representations within the deeper levels of [his] psyche…"[186]

Freud: (Surprised.) What? How could you miss them?

Boss: I've been thinking that "[i]f we do not, *a priori*…make an assumption of psychic entities in the patient about which…we neither have nor ever can have

---

[186] Boss, *Psychoanalysis and Daseinsanalysis*, 11.

any knowledge…then the reality of the patient indicates something quite other than what psychiatry and psychology would have us believe up until now."[187]

Freud: (Shaking his head in disappointment.) In other words, you are becoming seduced by your patient!

Boss: No, this is not about counter-transference. It is about a new way of thinking, a rethinking of psychoanalysis…

Freud: (Shakes his head.) Your objectivity is slipping away from you. How can you help this Professor Heidegger if you allow your own complexes and internal resistances to persist?

Boss: (Childishly.) Well, you obviously don't approve.

Freud: (Raised eyebrow.) I think you may be projecting here…I am, after all, merely a figment of your imagination…

Boss: Yes, well…(Clears throat.) If I recall, you were not always capable of escaping the dangers of counter-transference either.

Freud: Hmmm…So our friend Doktor Binswanger tattled on me, did he? It is true that we both struggled with this issue. "I regard[ed] it as more easily solvable on the theoretical level."[188] But keep in mind, those were private letters, between friends and colleagues…an appropriate place to voice one's concerns. I never intended those letters to be used as a rationalization for future analysts.

Boss: (Crossing arms.) Yes, well. I'm no longer convinced that objectivity and neutrality are essential to the therapeutic process.

Freud: (Suspicious.) Really?

Boss: I have come to believe that "'counter-transference' is not transference at all, but a genuine emotional inter-human relationship between the analyst and his patient…" In truth, "[a]n emotional relationship with the analysand can never be avoided by the analyst; it can only be denied by him."[189]

Freud: Did you feel I denied you my affection when you were my analysand? Is that what this is about?

---

[187] Ibid., 11-12.

[188] Ludwig Binswanger, *Sigmund Freud: Reminiscences of a Friendship*, trans. Norbert Guterman (New York and London, 1957), 50.

[189] Boss, *Psychoanalysis and Daseinsanalysis*, 258.

Boss: (Uncrossing his arms.) No, not at all. I actually found you to be quite gentle and kind.[190] You were a good father figure to me.

Freud: Then as your father, I must warn you that you are treading in dangerous waters. This is perhaps why you still need me? You want me to disapprove of your behavior?

Boss: (Surprised.) No, of course not. I think you are still here because of my concerns regarding the future of psychoanalysis.

Freud: (Curious and suspicious.) Oh? And what are your concerns?

Boss: I fear that the world will reject psychoanalysis in time…that would be a shame. But if we could come up with a way of grounding your therapy in some other philosophical tradition, something more humanistic, I believe that all your therapeutic work would be saved, even expanded and reapplied in fresh new ways.

Freud: (Not terribly happy.)   You sound a bit like our friend Doktor Binswanger. Is that what you have in mind? (Looks suspiciously at Boss.) Have you become so love struck by your dear Professor Heidegger that you wish to restore his broken reputation? Or have you found a launching pad from which you can ascend to your own glory as the founder of a new psychology?

Boss: (Stuttering a bit.) Hmmm, no, that's not it…

Freud: (Shakes his head.) All my disciples have left me to graze in fairer pastures…

Boss: (Interrupting.) It's just that it seems to me Professor Heidegger's insights could restore the original meaning and content of your "actual, immediate, concrete and brilliant observations…"[191]

Freud: (Still not happy.) Restore? Really?! If the task is to restore a dwelling, shouldn't one first shine his light in the basement? Restoring the above apartment is futile when the foundation is crumbling from neglect.[192]

Boss: I've just been thinking…

---

[190] This information was revealed to the authors of this play during a visit with Medard Boss in 1989.
[191] Boss, *Psychoanalysis and Daseinsanalysis*, 59.
[192] Binswanger, *Being-in-the-World*, 4.

Freud: (Muttering.)…Well, there's your problem.

Boss: (Continues uninterrupted.)…that in your work, one can discern two distinct ways of understanding humans…your therapeutic practice is opposed to your metapsychological theory so that at times they involve clear-cut contradictions.[193] It's as though there are really two "Freuds" within a philosophically split personality.

Freud: (Angrily.) Nonsense!

Boss: Please don't misunderstand me. I believe that your philosophically split personality does not denigrate psychoanalysis in any way.[194]

Freud: (Sarcastically.) Really?

Boss: The practical advice you give to analysts contains the same basic terms Professor Heidegger uses to describe human beings—There is thus an intrinsic harmony between the two.[195]

Freud: Harmony? (Shakes head.) I'm not sure we share the same taste in music.

Boss: Take, for example, Professor Heidegger's notion of "anticipatory care." His ideas are nearly identical to your own practical advice to psychotherapists! Like you, he distinguishes between "intervening care," and what he calls "leaping ahead" of another where a person "helps the Other to become transparent to himself *in* his care and to become *free for* it."[196]

Freud: I doubt this to be a secret to any of us who exhibit integrity in our interactions with others.

Boss: But you both see this very clearly…It is a distinct point of agreement. And both you and Professor Heidegger describe human existence in terms of "uncovering," "meaningfulness," "truths," "freedom"…while doing so, you both are talking about the same phenomena in the same way.[197]

Freud: (Shakes head.) I very much doubt that to be the case.

---

[193] Boss, *Psychoanalysis and Daseinsanalysis*, 58.
[194] Ibid., 61.
[195] Ibid.
[196] Heidegger, *Being and Time*, 158-59; see also Boss, *Psychoanalysis and Daseinsanalysis,* 74.
[197] Boss, *Psychoanalysis and Daseinsanalysis*, 61.

Boss: (Sits forward in his chair.) Take your fundamental rule of therapy; the goal is to enable the analysand to unveil himself. By doing so, you must have had a tacit awareness of human existence as an openness into which something can unveil itself from out of the dark.[198]

Freud: (Leans forward to meet Boss' gaze.) As you know…(Stares at him) and I know you know this…what I had in mind was allowing the analysand full freedom of expression so that the unconscious energies could more easily make their way into consciousness.

Boss: (Breaks Freud's gaze, but still excited.) But the same basic rule implies an idea of truth as "the shining forth of…unveiled phenomena…"[199]

Freud: (Loudly.) Mysticism! You sound as though you're chanting a Vedic hymn, not conducting science.[200]

Boss: (Staring at Freud. Pause.) In your analysis of dreams you showed that all human phenomena are meaningful which could be made sense of in the sequence of "the mental activities of waking life."[201]

Freud: (More calm.) Yes…So? Is that what Professor Heidegger is trying to say? I suppose that even he is bound to get some things right, (muttering) even if he is a philosopher.

Boss: (Encouraged.) Yes! And you might be surprised to discover that you both share a "common underlying conception of human freedom." It consists of man's capacity to choose his possibilities of relating to what he encounters or not.[202]

Freud: (Quietly, shaking his head.) No, you have misunderstood…

---

[198] Ibid., 62.

[199] Ibid.

[200] This makes reference to Freud's interest in Hinduism. See T. G. Vaidyanathan, and Jeffrey J. Kripal, eds., *Vishnu on Freud's Desk: A Reader in Psychoanalysis and Hinduism* (Delhi: Oxford University Press, 1999).

[201] Boss, *Psychoanalysis and Daseinsanalysis*, 65.

[202] Ibid., 67. It is important to note that Boss erroneously equates Heidegger's ontological conception of freedom (i.e., as openness) with Freud's more ontic everyday notion of freedom (i.e., as free to make a choice among alternatives). Boss was speaking merely of the derivative existential notion of freedom in Heidegger.

Boss: (Insistent.) I don't believe I have...while freely associating, you say that the analysand must have the capacity to choose to allow meanings to surface without censoring them.[203]

Freud: (Shaking head.) No, no, no...

Boss: But your own writings on therapeutic technique "abound with references to 'freedom'" which are grossly different from the deterministic viewpoint you hold in your metapsychology.[204]

Freud: (In a low tone.) You are mistaken.

Boss: I don't think so! (Pause.)

Freud: (Takes a deep breath. Looks down at the floor.) I was concerned when I wrote my therapeutic papers that such misunderstandings would emerge. (Faces Boss.) Look, you use your terms like "freedom" and "choice" all too loosely. But they are just words. Nothing more! Don't take them out of context! What you call a "philosophical split" is nothing more than the distinction one must make between a therapeutic procedure and a theoretical investigation! The two "cannot be carried out in the same way."[205] That is all you have unveiled here... The magician removes his robe and the rabbit is gone. There is no real magic in that...

Boss: (Resigned and dejected.) So you don't see it?

Freud: (Sternly confronting Boss.) What I see is a man who is tangled inside his own complexes, unwilling to examine his own motivations. Let us be perfectly clear on this subject; I consider your so-called work to be simply "an abandonment of analysis and a secession from it."[206] How dare you present yourself to me as my savior, when what you really are, is just another traitor to psychoanalysis? (Shakes finger at Boss.) Shame on you! And these ideas of yours...they are utterly absurd! Indeed, a betrayal!

Boss: (Quietly, but insistent.) I have no intention of betraying you, but I do believe that there is something quite valuable in Professor Heidegger's

---

[203] Boss, *Psychoanalysis and Daseinsanalysis*, 68.

[204] Ibid., 67. "Abound" is a bit of an overstatement. Boss only references three short passages that include the word "freedom" in Freud's therapeutic papers. However, these usages of "freedom" by Freud did not necessarily mean the existential freedom to which Boss refers. More likely, what Freud had in mind was the "freeing up" of libidinal energies in the unconscious. For a more extensive discussion, see Askay and Farquhar, *Apprehending the Inaccessible,* 325-32.

[205] Freud, *SE* XI, 142.

[206] Freud, *SE* XIV, 66.

philosophy that could humanize psychoanalysis (Looks at Freud reassuringly.) Just the theory, not your therapeutic practice…

Freud: (Stands up abruptly.) You ignorant fool, the two are unified! It is my metapsychology that demonstrates their unity! You cannot destroy one and expect the other to remain standing[207]…

Boss: (Looking up at Freud, defensively.) But you haven't even seriously considered Professor Heidegger's philosophy…

Freud: (Paces.) Oh, I have considered it…(Stops and looks at Boss.) Your great Professor Heidegger is a man torn between two separate worlds—the ontic world where every decision he has made, every action he has taken becomes a "mistake"—and what he calls "the ontological world" where his mind must live in order to avoid any responsibility…He uses his ontological analysis to avoid responsibility for his life…his poor decisions.

Boss: (Stands up facing Freud.) No, that is not what Professor Heidegger means in his discussion of the ontic and the ontological. The two are inseparable. The ontological is the deeper level of meaning from which the ontic is made possible.[208]

Freud: That may be what he says, but what is really occurring here is a philosophical rationalization. Can't you see that? Look, in your last session, when you were in therapy with Professor Heidegger, didn't you notice that when you mentioned the possibility of "fear," he immediately escaped into a philosophical discussion on "angst?"

Boss: (Goes back to his couch and sits down.) Yes, he was obviously resistant. I know that.

Freud: (Freud sits as well.) Well, angst is acceptable to him because it exists on the ontological level where fear cannot touch him.

Boss: He is only beginning to open up to me. I did not want to confront him and lose the trust I had gained.

Freud: I understand that. It was good not to pressure him, not to force your theories on him. But you do see how he uses his philosophical views of the ontological to avoid an authentic awareness of what is truly going on in his everyday existence?

---

[207] Freud, *SE* XIV, 78; 105; 222n.
[208] For a discussion on the "ontological difference," see Heidegger, *Zollikon Seminars*, 31; 192; 321-24.

Boss: Yes, I agree with you. It is peculiar how he says that focusing on the inauthenticity of fear conceals the underlying ontological basis for authenticity in angst, yet in his own life, he does just the reverse.

Freud: No doubt!

Boss: (Looking at Freud.) But he is not a well man...and just because he is avoiding his own fears, it doesn't negate the importance of his philosophy...In fact, his very confusion substantiates the truth he expounds in his philosophy!

Freud: How can it?

Boss: (Stands up pacing, shaking his head.) You don't know. You don't even understand his philosophical worldview.

Freud: What I do understand is that he uses his philosophy as a concealment—as he himself puts it—for his inability to accept his own erotic desires. Herr Doktor, this is a textbook case! Can't you see that?

Boss: (Stops pacing.) No, it can't be...

Freud: (Stands up behind Boss, as though he is talking in his ear. Boss faces audience.) Look, the man grows up in a highly restrictive religious environment, one that is "...characterized by its inordinate zeal for mortification of the flesh..."[209] He represses any and all erotic urges, proceeds to sublimate his unconscious energies in socially appropriate ambitions...and fails miserably. Why? Because his focus is exclusively in the intellect...he denies his unconscious desires...

Boss: (Shakes head in protest.) No, it isn't a matter of unconscious desires...

Freud: Of course it is...(Pauses. Turns to face Boss.) Remember his recurring dream?

Boss: (Stutters a bit.) Do you mean the one where his professors harassed him during his exams?

Freud: Yes, that's the one...(Gives Boss an odd look because it should be obvious.) He did say that was the only recurring dream he ever had, and continues to have, did he not?

Boss: (Feeling a bit stupid.) Oh, yes, of course. What do you make of that?

---

[209] Boss, *Psychoanalysis and Daseinsanalysis*, 5.

Freud: (Walks over to the chair and sits down.) Dreams of "matriculation examinations leave a certain obstinacy…"[210]

Boss: (Sits down on the couch, facing Freud.) That is certainly true in Professor Heidegger's case.

Freud: (Puts his cigar in his mouth.) Well, they "occur whenever, the person having done something wrong or failed to do something properly…expect(s) to be punished by the event…"[211]

Boss: Yes, I told him that's what you would say…

Freud: (Twirls cigar and looks at Boss.) I know you did, but it is interesting what you did not tell him.

Boss: Oh?

Freud: As you know, in my examinations of these particular types of dreams, I discovered that in saying "I'm a doctor, [or I'm a professor]…does not merely conceal a consolation but also signifies a reproach."[212]

Boss: (Confused.) In what way?

Freud: Well, in such a reproach, one is telling oneself, "You're quite old now, quite far advanced in life, and yet you go on doing these stupid, childish things."[213]

Boss: You think Professor Heidegger is condemning his behavior as childish? Is that what you are saying?

Freud: To some extent, yes…But it is "not surprising if the self-reproaches for being 'stupid' and 'childish' referred to other repetitions of reprehensible sexual acts."[214]

Boss: (Shocked. Sits up straight in his chair.) That is utterly absurd! Why would you say that?

Freud: (Quizzically.) Is it? Is it truly so absurd?

---

[210] Freud, *SE* IV, 273.
[211] Ibid., 274.
[212] Ibid., 275.
[213] Ibid., 275-76.
[214] Ibid., 276.

Boss: (Stands up and begins pacing.) Yes, of course it is absurd!

Freud: (Pause as he observes Boss' behavior.) Hmmmm…Who is Hannah Arendt?

Boss: (Stops pacing.) His lover…

Freud: She isn't just a woman…she is a *Jewess*…

Boss: No, it has nothing to do with his Nazism, that was just a bad decision on his part, a weakness in him to try to cope with the they-self mentality. But once he discovered the depth of what they were doing, he withdrew himself from public politics.[215]

Freud: I'm not talking about his Nazism here…What I am saying is that Hannah Arendt was not just a woman, she represented to Professor Heidegger all that was forbidden…all he could not admit into consciousness…She was, as he put it, "his soul," or as we would say, his unconscious, his id…

Boss: (Shaking head.) No, I cannot allow you to shrink Professor Heidegger into an object to prove your theories. They don't fit here.

Freud: They fit quite well, and you know this…His spies…they perfectly represent our super-ego…and his ego, well it is quite obvious that his ego is weakened but brilliant, especially in its ability to conceal and repress…He has managed to create an entire philosophy to avoid dealing with his repressed urges!

Boss: (Getting angry.) No, you don't understand…

Freud: (Takes out his notepad and begins writing in it.) And let us not fail to recognize the obvious indications of the Oedipus complex throughout his life struggles, for and against authority…

Boss: (Very angry now. Steps forward, away from Freud who sits behind him.) No! That's enough now!

---

[215] The circumstances surrounding Heidegger's participation in the Nazi party are, at best, unclear and ambiguous. There were numerous conflicting forces (some personal and some public) operating from a historical point of view which serve to obnubulate the matter—and yet within this tumultuous maelstrom, Heidegger's own actions in this imbroglio were clearly and undeniably normatively problematic, at least at times. However, Boss—as a close friend and colleague—defended Heidegger, saying that he had "indeed made some initial 'worldly innocent' misjudgments and mistakes." (Heidegger, *Zollikon Seminars*, xvi.)

(A moment of silence. BOSS looks down at the floor.)

Freud: (LIGHTS ON FREUD BEGIN TO FADE. He continues to write on his notepad.)   Hmmm.   You seem quite defensive.   (Pause.) Have I inadvertently stumbled upon the very issue you are having with your beloved Professor Heidegger?

Boss: (Loudly.) SILENCE! I will have no more of this!

Freud: (Voice fades.) ...Perhaps he is my replacement?

Boss: (As if addressing voices in his head.) No! Go away! You aren't even real! Just go! Let me be...

(LIGHTS OUT on FREUD. LIGHTS intensify on BOSS who is standing alone now. He is silent for a moment. He shakes his head; BOSS walks over to his desk where there is a photo of FREUD. BOSS picks up Freud's picture and looks at it for a bit. BOSS opens his desk drawer, places Freud's photo inside, and closes the drawer. BOSS reaches into his briefcase that is sitting beside the desk, and pulls out a photo of HEIDEGGER and BOSS. BOSS looks at this new photo for a moment then places it on his desk where the photo of FREUD was once placed.)

LIGHTS FADE

END OF PLAY

PART II

A Disclosure of Martin Heidegger, Medard Boss, and Sigmund Freud

One

On the Nature of Humans:
Sigmund Freud

For better or worse, Sigmund Freud's impact on Western civilization is undeniable. Some might even say that his theory of human nature permanently altered the way in which we conceive human beings. What many fail to recognize, however, is that Freud's intellectual development was a culmination of many generations of powerful ideas throughout the span of history, from Empedocles to the great thinkers present during his own lifetime. Even his scientific worldview, or "Weltanschauung," originated in the philosophical ideas embedded in the Enlightenment period. Thus, although he considered himself firmly rooted in the methodology of science, the many references to a huge array of historical ideas throughout his work reveals a deep thinker and creative synthesizer who sought to merge the two worlds of philosophy—which he considered speculative—and science—a method for genuine knowledge and change—into a psychoanalytic theory and practice.

Freud's relatively extensive exposure to philosophy as well as his commitment to psychiatry gave him an appreciation for both disciplines. At its best, he thought, philosophy illustrates the greatness to which humans can aspire in their endeavors to wrestle with tensions between self and the external world. He was fascinated by the superior intelligences of philosophers, and what they could offer toward a more penetrating insight into human reality. However, he also viewed philosophy from within his own paradigm of psychological thinking. Philosophy was a superb example of successful sublimation—the redirecting of powerful instinctual energies into socially acceptable channels. Hence, although he admired and made use of a wealth of philosophical ideas, he also did so from the standpoint of a more basic understanding of primitive human nature. He thought that psychoanalysis was quite prepared to uncover the inner workings of even the greatest of minds. His "psychography" could expose and demonstrate the psychical motives operating beneath the intellects of philosophers who develop their impressive theories. Such motives, he was convinced, were essentially the same subjective motives fundamental to all human mental functioning. For example, philosophical worldviews—when used as a means of defense—can be viewed not just as a form of sublimation, but also as "reaction formations," (i.e., "exaggerations of the normal traits of character").[1] It is possible that

---

[1] Freud, *SE* XX, 157. It is important to note that "reaction formation" can also take the form of "intensifying an opposite." (*SE* XIV, 157) For example, a sadistic tendency

some philosophers create elaborate intellectual theories to deny or conceal their own most basic urges.[2] Hence, although philosophy purports to offer logical and impartial theories to explain human existence, such theories are still rooted in human instinctual history.

It is worth mentioning that Freud's original academic goal was to take his advanced degrees in both philosophy and zoology. His theory and practice reflect such interests. Consistent with Darwinian and Lamarkian evolutionary theory, Freud considered humans as a particular species of animal. Obviously, he was not easily seduced by the advancement of thought within the higher intellectual realms. His focus was always on the organic substructures of the human organism, and the breakdown in mental functioning that so often resulted in disturbances of both body and mind in the patients he sought to treat. Psychiatry proved to be the ideal field of inquiry. It was here that he witnessed blindness in perfectly functioning eyes, paralysis in healthy limbs, and so forth. Contrary to many doctors of the time, Freud acknowledged that these patients were not "faking it." Rather, something else must be the cause. Knowing that the mind is a powerful force in health and illness, Freud focused his attention on human mental functioning. His hope was ultimately to offer a means for curing the ailments of mental suffering in individuals, to expose the forces that plague society, and to elucidate the dynamic tensions between the two.

PSYCHOANALYSIS AND METAPSYCHOLOGICAL THEORY

Freud's psychoanalysis consisted of a number of diverse, yet interrelated components; it was a research procedure, a therapeutic method, and a collection of psychological information, all of which existed as a unified scientific endeavor.[3] His theory, upon which his therapy was based, was

---

can be repressed, and manifested as overly affectionate toward the object toward which one feels hostile. Ibid., 156; see also Freud, *SE* XIV, 281.

[2] Freud also speculated, "social order, morals, justice and religion had arisen together in the primaeval ages of mankind as reaction-formations against the Oedipus complex." Freud, *SE* XVIII, 253.

[3] Note that Medard Boss and others contended that Freud was split between his theory and practice. It is our contention that Freud would have opposed this idea. In discussing his therapeutic practice and why certain phenomena seem to hold, Freud wrote, "If we are asked by what methods and means this result is achieved, it is not easy to find an answer. We can only say: 'We must call the Witch to our help after all!' [This in reference to a quote from Goethe, *Faust*, Part I, Scene 6]—The Witch Metapsychology. Without metapsychological speculation and theorizing—I had almost said 'phantasying'—we shall not get another step forward." Freud, *SE* XXIII, 225. On the next page, Freud footnoted that "It is impossible to define health except in metapsychological terms: i.e. by reference to the dynamic relations between the agencies of the mental apparatus which have been recognized—or (if that is preferred) inferred or conjectured—by us." Freud, *SE* XXIII, 226 n2. A perusal of Freud's work, we believe, substantiates that psychoanalysis was a unified science, and any so-called

deemed *"meta*psychology."[4]   It would provide the ground for all possible meaning, including philosophy. For although he believed that psychoanalysis as a science was constructed through and remained committed to empirical observation, at times he transcended the limits of pure science in order to make sense of psychical processes more adequately.   In justifying his metapsychological concept of the unconscious, for example, Freud wrote: "A gain in meaning is a perfectly justifiable ground for going beyond the limits of direct experience."[5] Freud's theory, then, is "meta" because psychoanalysis required a non-empirical—albeit scientific—foundation.

Freud was quite explicit in defining his metapsychological theory: "it is a method of approach according to which every mental process is considered in relation to three coordinates, which I described as *dynamic, topographic*, and *economic*."[6]   All three coordinates were regarded as interrelated, but provided unique standpoints from which to view mental functioning.

Briefly, the *dynamic* component considers all mental processes (except those that are received directly from external stimuli) as an interplay of forces. Energies within the body combine and divide, assist and inhibit one another, creating mental images and ideas with an affective force and power. These forces originate in the instincts and hence have an organic basis. Freud believed that human instincts were of two basic groups, the "ego-instincts" which are concerned with issues of self-preservation, and the "object-instincts," which are directed outwardly to the external world. Behind the manifest ego-instincts and object-instincts were what Freud termed "Eros" (i.e., "libidinal energies"), and "Thanatos" (i.e., the "death instinct"). Eros as a unifying force seeks to combine and restore what is lost; while Thanatos, as a destructive force, seeks to dissolve.[7] In this constant coming together and tearing apart, there is a conservation of energies that is characteristic of the instincts. It is exemplified by the phenomenon of a *compulsion to repeat*: fish return to their spawning grounds, birds migrate, humans perpetually repeat destructive patterns that apparently run counter to their best interests. These patterns of behavior, according to Freud, demonstrate the underlying conflicting forces of the instincts. "The picture which life presents to us is the result of the concurrent and mutually opposing action of Eros and the death

---

split is unjustifiable. See also, Askay and Farquhar, *Apprehending the Inaccessible,* 325-32.

[4] It would provide the ground for all possible meaning, including philosophy. This is why Freud took it as one of his goals "to transform metaphysics into metapsychology." Freud, *SE* VI, 259.

[5] Freud, *SE* XIV, 167.

[6] Freud, *SE* XX, 59.

[7] Freud, *SE* XX, 265.

instinct."[8]   All life wishes for an ultimate reduction in tension, to return once again to that inorganic state from which it emerged.[9]

The *economic* standpoint stipulates that the mental representations of the instincts, for example, images, ideas and thoughts, have an affective charge (cathexis) of definite quantities of energy. The mind seeks to regulate these energies and keep the excitations at a low level, operating according to the "pleasure-unpleasure principle." When tensions begin to build (unpleasure), the mental system seeks to discharge these energies, and reduce them to a balanced state (pleasure). On the level of infantile functioning, for example, a baby experiences discomfort and cries. If the cause is hunger, the crying indicates a need for food (tension and unpleasure); when fed, that need is satisfied and crying stops (pleasure). Tensions have been reduced; the body returns to its natural state of equilibrium. In the course of development, the original *pleasure principle* undergoes modifications due to its interactions with the external world. Experience leads to the "*reality principle*," where the mind is better equipped to postpone immediate pleasure and tolerate temporary feelings of unpleasure.[10]

In addition, Freud's *topographical* account of mental functioning specifies where various mental processes take place. He did not intend this as an actual location in space, but rather a description of how the mind operates, and the particular focus of various energies.[11]   The mental apparatus, according to Freud, is composed of an "*id*," "*ego*," and a "*super-ego*." The *id* is basically a repository of the instinctual impulses, the reservoir of libidinal energies.[12] "It is the dark, inaccessible part of our personality... a cauldron full of seething excitations...It is filled with energy reaching it from the instincts, but it has no organization, produces no collective will, but only a striving to bring about the satisfaction of the instinctual needs subject to the observance of the pleasure principle."[13] The id is what is first developed in humans—the instinctual pool from which the ego and super-ego evolve. As the normal human begins to mature, she or he is forced to interact more with the external world to satisfy innate urges. External stimulations interact with perceptions and instincts as the *ego* begins to form on the exterior layers of the id. Yet, as a modification of the id, the instincts continue to exert an important influence on the ego. The ego becomes something akin to a mediator, working to satisfy the internal libidinal energies of the id while avoiding retribution from the outside world. It is essentially a defense against threatening forces as well as a means for survival. Through conflict and experience with the external world, the ego creates the *super-ego* from the id. The super-ego is

---

[8] Freud, *SE* XX, 57.
[9] Freud, *SE* XXII 106-7.
[10] Freud, *SE* XX, 266.
[11] Freud, *SE* XXIII, 97.
[12] Freud, *SE* XX 266; *SE* XIX, 30n1.
[13] Freud, *SE* XXII, 73.

ultimately an internalization of family values and social/cultural rules. As Freud conceives it, "the ego, driven by the id, confined by the super-ego, repulsed by reality, struggles to master its economic task of bringing about harmony among the forces and influences working in and upon it…"[14]

Freud's topographical account has another dimension, that of *unconsciousness* and *consciousness*. Both the ego and super-ego operate within consciousness and unconsciousness. The id, however, is strictly unconscious. Given that the ego originates and develops from the id, most of mental activity occurs on the level of unconsciousness. However, at times some images and thoughts surface to the level of preconscious awareness. When this occurs, the ego gains access to such material and can bring it into consciousness. Conscious ideas and thoughts only remain conscious for a brief time before they sink into latency. Thoughts that can easily become conscious again are considered "*preconscious*;"[15] those that sink below all access—for example, censored and rejected as a defensive maneuver—return once again to the unconscious id. When this occurs, thoughts are said to have undergone *repression*. "Here then is the 'repressed' in the id…unconscious processes in the id are raised to the level of the preconscious and incorporated into the ego, and that, on the other hand, preconscious material in the ego can follow the opposite path and be put back into the id…"[16] Information from the external world can also enter into consciousness. The ego works it over and can retain it on the preconscious level, or reject it, allowing it to slip into unconsciousness.

It should be stressed, that Freud believes that no one truly forgets.[17] We can suppress thoughts and ideas while still having access, or we can repress them to the point of restricted access, or no access at all. But each thought, each idea once created or experienced is forever stored in unconsciousness unless it can gain access to the preconscious thereby becoming a possibility for consciousness. This includes everyday experiences that eventually descend into latency,[18] childhood memories, and even archaic memory-traces from past generations, brought to us through our genetic heritage.[19] Hence, although it may appear that memories simply fade with time, Freud rejects this idea. He specifically states: "It is highly probable that there is no question at all of there being any direct function of time in

---

[14] Freud, *SE* XXII, 78.

[15] Freud, *SE* XXII, 70.

[16] Freud, *SE* XXIII 96-97.

[17] Freud writes, "…it is our belief that no one forgets anything without some secret reason or hidden motive." Freud, *SE* IX, 22.

[18] It is important to add that unimportant thoughts cannot be "forgotten" although they do undergo condensation. Condensation is a natural function of the instincts that serve to conserve energies. Freud, *SE* VI, 274n2.

[19] This is a reference to Freud's position on phylogenetic heritage. See Askay and Farquhar, *Apprehending the Inaccessible,* xii, 30, 36, 37, 61, 64, 110, 127, 238, 343, 349, 373 for a more in depth discussion.

forgetting."[20] For Freud, the unconscious is "timeless." This he concluded after repeated confirmation from his numerous years of experience and investigations.   When   unconscious   memories   were   accessed   via psychoanalysis, Freud found "that they undergo no alteration even in the course of the longest period of time."[21] What was perhaps most surprising was that "all impressions are preserved, not only in the same form in which they were first received, but also in all the forms which they adopted in their further developments."[22]   Every detail of events, from the most important to the apparently least significant, are retained and potentially recalled, as are the later connections one acquires regarding such events. Freud's position on "forgetting"—or rather the impossibility of it—is vital in understanding his theoretical constructions. He believed that neurotic symptoms had their roots in unconscious childhood memories—all repression takes place during the most formative years.[23] Until those unconscious memories are allowed access into preconsciousness thereby becoming possible for consciousness, disturbed mental functioning is bound to its pathology.

Given the emphasis on early childhood, it is important to consider briefly aspects of Freud's developmental theory. Freud observed that all infants take their nourishment from some source. Most often in Freud's time, mothers nursed their babies.[24] Freud stipulated that newborn babies are pure id; they are incapable of making the distinction between the mother's breast and their own bodies—all sensations are internal with no awareness of an external world. It is only through a gradual process of physiological (bodily and mental) development that infants come to recognize a world external to self. As the child begins to develop, the mother's breast becomes recognizable as an external object—a "love object"—but it is only a breast. Eventually the baby is capable of conceiving a whole person—the mother. This original separation of self and mother is the initial conflict that all humans must endure; Eros, the unifying instinct, comes into conflict with a world that is not within one's control.

Separation from the mother as an external object leads to identification. The child seeks to possess the mother, to return to that natural state of unity. Possessing the mother becomes sexual as the child develops, because the instincts, as self-preserving energies that desire unification, begin to be experienced in the bodily realms, including the genital areas. In addition, the father becomes recognizable as an external object. His authoritative role in the family as well as his possession of the mother are seen as threatening—he

---

[20] Freud, *SE* VI, 274n2.

[21] Freud, *SE* VI, 274n2.

[22] Freud, *SE* VI, 274n2.

[23] Freud, *SE* XXIII, 227.

[24] Freud discussed bottle fed babies as well, but saw little difference in the impact of feedings on development. Whether by bottle or breast, babies still most often fed from their mothers.

becomes a potential impediment to securing instinctual satisfaction and survival.[25] Such a threat requires a defensive maneuver on the part of the child—identification thus occurs as the primary mode of mitigating any perceived dangers from parental figures. Freud believed that all children must grapple with subsequent issues of hatred and/or ambivalence toward the father, and conflicting emotions toward the mother. The process of conflict and resolution during these formative years is what Freud deemed the *Oedipus complex*.

The term "Oedipus complex" was taken from an ancient Greek legend of King Oedipus—an unfortunate hero who unwittingly killed his father and married his mother. Freud considered this legend historical evidence for a repetitive theme (a compulsion to repeat) that permeates all of humanity and represents a universal inevitability.[26] The repulsion and rejection many people feel upon learning about Freud's Oedipus complex assent to its unconscious and repressed nature. Yet, it is out of this fundamental conflict, Freud insists, that humans gradually develop their cultural identities and are able to function normally in society; from the resolution of the Oedipus complex the super-ego develops. "The reactions against the instinctual demands of the Oedipus complex are the source of the most precious and socially important achievements of the human mind; and this holds true not only in the life of individuals but probably also in the history of the human species as a whole. The super-ego, too, the moral agency which dominates the ego, has its origin in the process of overcoming the Oedipus complex."[27]

In the process of resolving the Oedipus complex, the child builds up various means of defense, usually within the first five years of development. Recall that it is the ego's primary task to mediate between the demands of the internal id and external world in accordance with the pleasure principle—to keep tensions at a comfortable level—and to protect the id from any perceived dangers. In so doing, the ego must censor internal and external information in order to fulfill its protective function. As Freud conceives it, "The psychical apparatus is intolerant of unpleasure; it has to fend it off at all costs, and if the perception of reality entails unpleasure, that perception—that is, the truth—

---

[25] Although Freud believed that females also undergo the Oedipus complex, his account was unsatisfactory in explaining female development. Freud made the fatal mistake of beginning with male development in constructing the Oedipus complex. He then attempted to fit female development into the same paradigm. Given that the two sexes are biologically and socially different, his explanations are severely tainted by his approach. Due to its extensive nature, this text does not discuss the descriptions and problems Freud creates, but seeks to explore the reasons for the Oedipus complex as a universal construction.

[26] Freud saw this theme in other historical material as well. For instance, Shakespeare's *Hamlet* represented an alternative version of the Oedipus complex.

[27] Freud, *SE* XX, 268.

must be sacrificed."[28]   The ego is thus actively engaged in mentally constructing a "reality" that supports its need for survival.

One way in which the ego creates reality is by means of *projection*. Freud points out that projection is not just a defense mechanism, because it exists even in cases where there is no apparent conflict—no threat to one's continued existence.   He writes, "The projection outwards of internal perceptions is a primitive mechanism, to which, for instance, our sense perceptions are subject, and which therefore normally plays a very large part in determining the form taken by our external world...internal perceptions of emotional and thought processes can be projected outwards in the same way as sense perceptions; they are thus employed for building up the external world, though they should by rights remain part of the *internal* world."[29]   Perhaps, Freud's theory of projection accounts for the conflict created in instances of human diversity—that is, in assuming (or projecting) that all other humans are essentially the same as ourselves, we are resistant to accepting differences, and instead attempt to force our own opinions, understandings, values, and so forth upon the rest of the world.

Interestingly, according to Freud, people tend to operate with a select few defense mechanisms that become "fixated" in the ego as "regular modes of reaction of...character."[30]   Because of the dynamic and economic nature of the mental system, these same defensive maneuvers are repeatedly applied (i.e., compulsion to repeat) in threatening situations throughout life.[31] Unfortunately, the original purpose of these defense mechanisms—to protect against "dangers, anxiety, and unpleasure"[32]—often persist even after threats to one's survival have been removed. At times, the adult ego will even "seek out those situations in reality which can serve as an approximate substitute for the original danger, so as to be able to justify, in relation to them, its maintaining its habitual modes of reaction."[33]   In other words, humans do not just react against internal and external worlds of perceived threats to survival; they actually seek out situations that reinforce repetitive patterns—experiences that have become familiar, and with which they are equipped to deal. Hence, defense mechanisms can eventually become dangers in themselves. They can serve to restrict a person's mode of relating to self, world, and others, weakening the ego in the process, and potentially initiating the "outbreak of neurosis."[34]

---

[28] Freud, *SE* XXIII, 237.
[29] Freud, *SE* XIII, 64.
[30] Freud, *SE* XXIII, 237. Anna Freud was the one who did an extensive analysis of the various defense mechanisms.
[31] Ibid.
[32] Ibid., 235.
[33] Ibid., 238.
[34] Ibid.

"FREEDOM" IN THERAPY

Given Freud's metapsychological theory, including its developmental factors, it is perhaps clear where he stood on the issue of human freedom. Humans are conceived as biologically determined. "Free will" itself is a biological fact of human existence; it is by virtue of human mental processes, which are grounded in physical instinctual impulses, that the conviction of free will truly exists. "Many people, as is well known, contest the assumption of complete psychical determinism by appealing to a special feeling of conviction that there is a free will. This feeling of conviction exists; and it does not give way before a belief in determinism…the feeling that we have is rather one of psychical compulsion…determinism in the psychical sphere is still carried out without any gap."[35] As with any psychical compulsion the therapist's role is not to dispute the existence of free will, but rather to understand the motivating force behind the compulsion. And like all compulsions, the feeling of free will originates in an instinctual need[36]—we desire to see ourselves as having choices, else we lose hope in our ability to control the forces within and around us in order to protect and preserve our existence.

Some believe that Freud's psychological determinism[37] undermines the very nature of the therapeutic process. For how can individuals choose therapy and eventually heal if there is no choice? Freud would most likely respond that the belief in choice and change could be motivating factors for psychotherapeutic success; therapists treat their patients "as if" they are free to inspire confidence in the possibility of a cure. In fact, Freud clearly states that the theory behind psychoanalysis should never be forced upon patients, and not revealed to them until they are ready. But there is a further point to be made. Psychopathology is not a natural state of being. The amount of energy required to repress unacceptable unconscious material from making its way into preconscious and conscious thought acts as a "dam against the pressure of water."[38] Because the instincts operate according to principles of conservation, there is only so much energy available for repression. Thus repression inhibits the dynamic system from being able to move freely. The "freedom" therapy affords suffering individuals is a freeing up of those blocked energies so that the ego can be restored. "We try to restore the ego, to

---

[35] Freud, *SE* VI, 253-54.

[36] Freud, *SE* VI, 253-54. For a more extensive discussion on Freud's "determinism" see Askay and Farquhar, *Apprehending the Inaccessible*, 328-36 where the authors argue that Freud was not fully aware of the ramifications of freedom versus determinism. Had he had a deeper understanding, he likely would have held a similar position to Schopenhauer's.

[37] Freud is considered to be a psychological determinist, rather than a strict determinist. He writes, "I believe in external (real) chance, it is true, but not in internal (psychical) accidental events." Freud, *SE* VI, 257. In other words, he does believe that there can be chance or random external events, but not unmotivated thoughts or actions.

[38] Freud, *SE* XXIII, 226.

free it from its restrictions and to give it back command over the id which it has lost owing to its early repressions."[39]

Consistent with his dynamic and economic views, Freud regards mental illness as an economical reaction to conflict and trauma—a person experiences a "flight into illness" because it is considered the most efficient way to protect oneself from perceived threats. "Falling ill involves a saving of psychical effort; it emerges as being economically the most convenient solution where there is a mental conflict...even though in most cases the ineffectiveness of such an escape becomes manifest at a later stage."[40] Even when the original threat is removed, the memory-trace of the threat remains. Awareness of the threat, however, must be repressed insofar as it continues to be viewed as a threat. Thus, in order to defend itself the ego's censor excludes all thoughts, ideas, and actions related to these unacceptable memories from gaining access to consciousness. There arises a tension between a person's failure to remember (conscious) and an impossibility to forget (unconscious). The more this tension swells, the more one must devote energies to the repression of the material. And the more the energies are held back or repressed, the more their tendency is to leak into alternative channels—producing "symptoms" of neurosis.[41]

Often times, what is most unacceptable and denied conscious access involves the sexual instinct. This is due, in part, to the cultural restrictions placed on children during their early development. Freud believes that many neurotic symptoms are substitutes for repressed sexuality, and are indicative of an unresolved Oedipus complex. When patients come to therapy, these unresolved parental issues get *transferred* onto the therapist. Patients develop emotional attachments to their therapists—whether affectionate (positive) or hostile (negative)—and it is this *transference*, when used properly (according to psychoanalytic insights), which allows therapists to help their patients overcome repression.[42] As Freud states it, "We have formulated our task as physicians thus: to bring to the patient's knowledge the unconscious, repressed impulses existing in him, and, for that purpose, to uncover the resistances that oppose this extension of his knowledge about himself."[43]

Obviously, patients come to therapy to heal. However, owing to the inadmissibility of unconscious memories into consciousness, patients are *resistant* to this process. As unconscious material begins to surface, the ego perceives recovery as a "new danger,"[44] and makes use of various procedures in order to defend itself.[45] These defense mechanisms reveal themselves in the

---

[39] Freud, *SE* XX, 205.
[40] Freud, *SE* VII, 43n.
[41] Freud, *SE* XX, 267.
[42] Freud, *SE* XX, 267.
[43] Freud, *SE* XVII, 159.
[44] Freud, *SE* XXIII, 238.
[45] Ibid., 235.

form of resistances to the therapeutic process.[46] Thus, such resistances can act as an appraisal of achievement—an indication that the therapist is coming closer to uncovering the unacceptable material that holds their patients captive. However, if patients become too resistant, therapy can become ineffectual. Thus, therapy is essentially a balancing act—to bring about gradual conscious awareness of repressed material without it becoming perceived as too great a threat to survival.[47] Ultimate success is measured in degrees; both by how much unconscious material is admitted into consciousness, and the extent to which symptoms permanently disappear. Previous compulsions must be "lifted" from the mind. "For conscious will-power governs only conscious mental processes, and every mental compulsion is rooted in the unconscious…It is only by the application of our highest mental functions, which are bound up with consciousness, that we can control all our impulses."[48]

PSYCHOTHERAPEUTIC TECHNIQUE

In the process of therapy, the analyst must remain "objective" and hold a neutral stance. This is imperative. By providing a blank screen, the unresolved issues a patient retains from early childhood inevitably transfer to the analyst. Recall that the developing infant first approaches the mother's breast as undifferentiated, and only later conceives of it as a "love object." If positive transference is successful, the patient will likewise conceive of the therapist as a love object—perhaps a father figure from the patient's tumultuous past—and will project his or her feelings toward that original love object onto the therapist. This is due, in part, to the condensation of instincts and the compulsion to repeat. For as we form our early perceptions and develop our ways of relating in the world, we do so out of a conservation of energies; strong emotional impulses gathered from a multitude of unpleasurable childhood experiences, condense and project outwardly onto an object of hatred, for example. Behaviors charged with the force of that hatred are repeated over and over again in what is perceived as connected experiences among similar encounters. Thus, trauma experienced within early relationships sets the course for later interactions. If perceived harm comes from the father, all men will represent the object "father" over the course of our lives, and we will unavoidably act consistently toward that object.

Ideally, therapists recognize these patterns of behavior and the necessary function of transference in the therapeutic process. When patients gives their affections, their therapists understand that this is a natural and necessary unfolding, an opportunity for therapeutic success. However, therapists themselves are human with their own unresolved childhood issues.

---

[46] Ibid., 238-39.
[47] Ibid., 240.
[48] Freud, *SE* VII, 266.

It is not an easy task to remain "objective" when patients pour their feelings of love onto their therapists. "Counter-transference" is more than likely to occur. It is for this reason that Freud insisted that it was imperative for all therapists to seek their own therapy. For therapists can only take their patients as far as they themselves are able to go. If counter-transference is acted out (e.g., in the creation of a loving, sexual relationship between analyst and analysand), therapists risk causing further damage to their vulnerable patients, negating the possibility for therapeutic progress.

Clearly Freud was aware that physicians were in a unique position of authority; for better or worse, the power of their suggestions could seriously impact the health of their patients. He urged all medical professionals to gain training in psychoanalysis, even those who dealt strictly with physiological ailments.[49] Quite obviously, the body is impacted by the mental states of all who suffer. This was demonstrated continuously early in Freud's career as he witnessed and employed methods of suggestion through the use of *hypnosis*. As if by magic, long standing illnesses of, for example, blindness and paralysis would simply disappear strictly by implanting a powerful suggestion. Unfortunately, as Freud later discovered, unless there is a process of working through—via the therapeutic process of converting repressed unconscious material into consciousness—other symptoms would develop as replacements for previous symptoms. Instead, what was necessary was a technique that would allow the unconscious energies of the patient to surface so that the analyst could facilitate the movement of these repressed energies into preconscious thought. It was with this in mind that Freud abandoned hypnosis (around 1896) and replaced it with "the fundamental rule" of free association.

Freud's therapeutic method of free association requires that the patient recline on a couch in order to get comfortable and relaxed.[50] The therapist sits off to the side of the patient, out of direct view and unobtrusive, taking on the role of an objective, non-judgmental blank screen upon which transference can take place. In addition, the patient must agree to the mandates of the fundamental rule—to tell the therapist everything, "not only what he can say intentionally and willingly, what will give him relief like a confession, but everything else as well that his self-observation yields him, everything that comes into his head, even if it is disagreeable for him to say it, even if it seems to him unimportant or actually nonsensical."[51] Given his metapsychological theory, the purpose of this technique is clear—to provide the conditions for freely flowing thoughts and ideas. Freud speculated that restricted thoughts with their roots in the unacceptable realms of unconsciousness would inevitably slip out, most likely in some distorted form. This is due to the dynamic and economic nature of the system. For the powerful dynamic energies underlying the thoughts cannot remain wholly

---

[49] Freud, *SE* VII, 258-59.
[50] Sitting across from a patient also represents an oppositional relationship.
[51] Freud, *SE* XXIII, 174.

pushed down; and a weakened ego under such stressful conditions as repression cannot be entirely successful in occluding these thoughts from escaping. Such insights were gleaned, confirmed, and elaborated upon by means of Freud's investigations into, for example, parapraxes, and his analysis of dreams.

By "parapraxes," Freud had in mind instances when we make apparently innocent errors in spite of knowing better, when we utter or write down the wrong word when we meant something different (i.e., "slips of the tongue or pen"), when we "bungle" an action we have successfully performed before, and so forth—all these unintended "mistakes" that upon being corrected, we excuse ourselves by attributing them to "chance," or "inattentiveness."[52] These are cases of "forgetting" that Freud found particularly interesting. For upon psychoanalytic investigation, he came to believe that such phenomena could be traced back to psychical material that was incompletely suppressed. Unconscious thoughts not allowed access to consciousness still managed to express themselves in these "accidents."[53] This supplied him with additional evidence in support of his psychological determinism, because he had shown that even those seemingly "chance" occurrences, received their motivating force from unconscious activity.[54]

Dream analysis[55] confirmed and further deepened Freud's understanding of mental functioning. He approached and defined dreams in terms of their biological function; the body sleeps out of a physiological necessity. However, just as in waking life, the mind is not completely at rest: external stimuli surrounds the sleeper, internal energies continue to flow, bodily sensations are still experienced, instinctual impulses from the id (e.g., hunger, sexual feelings, etc.) persist, and so forth. In other words, even in sleep the ego encounters a multitude of demands that must be satisfied in order to allow the body to rest deeply. If this were not the case, if the body could

---

[52] Freud, *SE* VI, 239-40.

[53] Freud, *SE* VI, 279.

[54] Freud, *SE* IX, 105.

[55] It is important to note that Freud's dream analysis consisted primarily of applying his technique of "free association" to the retelling of dreams. The interpretation of a patient's dreams were to be evaluated in terms of the entire historical context of the patient—and it was primarily up to the patient to discern the "correct fit" for the therapist's interpretations: "…it is the dreamer himself who should tell us what his dream means." (Freud, *SE* XV, 101.) In the process of Freud's investigations into dreams, certain elements surfaced that resisted individual interpretation and appeared to be universal among all patients. These were few in number. However, according to Freud such elements represented *universal symbols* common to all humans and embedded in the phylogenetic history of humankind. (Freud, *SE* IV, 264; *SE* XIII; *SE* XV, 207-8; *SE* XVII, 261-62; *SE* XX, 68; *SE* XXI, 252; *SE* XXIII, esp. 192.) Despite this intriguing finding, Freud warned against "over-estimating the importance of symbols in dream-interpretation," (Freud, *SE* V, 359-60) and insisted that these universal symbols were to be considered a "supplement" only to the much broader process of dream interpretation. (Freud, *SE* XV, 151.)

simply shut down or turn off, dreams would not be necessary. However, because the ego must continue to deal with external, internal, and psychical stimuli, it persists in performing its tasks, although not as skillfully as it does during the waking state because the ego too is relaxed. Its censoring function is not as acute.

The purpose of dreams, according to Freud, is to maintain sleep. *"Dreams are the* GUARDIANS *of sleep and not its disturbers."*[56] They are the images that the ego creates in order to satisfy the demands imposed upon it while the body rests. In this sense, dreams are wish-fulfillments. If the body is hungry, for example, the dream of food temporarily fulfills the wish to eat; if there is a crash from outside, the dream creates an image to assure the dreamer that it is of no concern. However, it is also the case that during sleep, the mind is focused primarily on internal stimuli—the dynamic forces of the instincts. The id, being the cauldron of seething desires makes itself more pronounced because attention is drawn internally, away from external distractions. Unconscious thoughts and ideas have a great deal more freedom, and this presents a problem for the ego. Its ability to censor information is not as discriminating, and the id gains more strength during this weakened state. However, these instinctual desires and traumatic memories are often times not at all acceptable to the conscious mind. Hence, when the ego creates the dream images, it must do so in such a way as to satisfy the id without offending consciousness. This is why Freud believed that there are two psychical forces operating in the formation of dreams: the creative force which creates the dream in order to satisfy desires and promote sleep, and the defensive force which distorts the dream in order to make the unconscious material more acceptable to the dreamer and protect the sleeping state. It is by censoring and distorting the dream that the ego is able to fulfill the wish of even the most abhorrent desires, all the while keeping the dreamer at rest. It should be mentioned that at times, the ego is unsuccessful in its attempts. A dream that is not distorted sufficiently escapes the censor, shocking the conscious mind, and resulting in the disruption of sleep. In such cases, it is clear that the ego has failed in its function.

Because of the distorted nature of dreams, Freud was clear that the psychotherapeutic approach to dreams must take into account both the *manifest* and *latent* content of dreams. The *manifest* content is what is readily apparent, the actual description of the dream, and what patients present during analysis. The manifest content utilizes recent experiences that can often be traced to the past few days' events. But the actual significance of the dream is to be found at a much deeper level. Borrowing from recent events, dream images are formed via their intimate connection to unconscious meanings, or *latent* content. What would otherwise be "indifferent material" left over from the past few days would not have the kind of force necessary for the creation of a dream—given that dreams only arise as a means to distort unacceptable

---

[56] Freud, *SE* VI, 267.

material and prolong sleep. Hence, the latent content must come from unconscious wishes that are suppressed or repressed—yet still active—during the waking state, and given more freedom. The work involved in transforming the latent thoughts into manifest dreams, that is, the "dream work," is limited to a few activities of the ego censor: condensation, displacement, representability, and secondary revision.

Briefly stated, *condensation* is the process by which the many events of the past days get condensed and organized according to their connectedness to unconscious material. *Displacement* is when the ego chooses a different object (one that does not have an "intensely cathected" emotional charge) to represent the unconscious material. *Representability* is the complex mental process of transforming thoughts—no matter how abstract—into dream images. And *secondary revision* is the working over of dream material to produce images that conform, more or less, to our categories of understanding. Dreams that undergo secondary revision appear to make sense whereas those aspects of dreams that have not undergone this process are confused and often times nonsensical.

To put these four features of "dream work" together in a simplified fashion, let us suppose that over the past few days, I greeted the postal person who had a laugh just like my father, saw the green flash of a traffic light—the color of my father's eyes—and heard the breaking of a twig like the sound of the "crack" of a ruler. All of these encounters went essentially unnoticed by my conscious mind. But during the course of the night I dream of a splinter of wood enclosed within a green envelope. This seemingly innocent manifest item actually represents a latently repressed childhood memory of having been beaten by my father with a ruler after being caught engaging in a forbidden sexual activity. None of this was in my conscious awareness, but through an application of free association during dream analysis, this unconscious material is able to surface into preconscious awareness.

What most fascinated Freud about parapraxes and dreams, is that they are both universal among humans, and not just an outcome of pathological thinking. Freud asserts, *"The interpretation of dreams is the royal road to a knowledge of the unconscious activities of the mind."*[57] For even in the "normal" person, dreams reveal the same basic aspects of mental functioning as in the neurotic. His extensive analysis of dreams and parapraxes justified his scientific assertions regarding unconsciousness. "The mechanism of parapraxes...can be seen to correspond in its most essential points with the mechanism of dream-formation...We have the same situation: by unfamiliar paths, and by the way of external associations, unconscious thoughts find expression as modifications of other thoughts."[58] Unconscious thoughts essentially ride piggyback on the traces of other thoughts, forming a web of interconnections that permeate all of human mental life. They are with us

---

[57] Freud, *SE* V, 608.
[58] Freud, *SE* VI, 278.

always, despite (and perhaps because of) our lack of awareness. Hence, not only are dreams and parapraxes a means for uncovering hidden meanings—a valuable psychotherapeutic tool—they also provide precious material from which Freud constructed and validated his universal theories of unconsciousness, and its relationship to complete mental functioning. In so doing, Freud came to realize "...the borderline between the normal and the abnormal in nervous matters is a fluid one...we are all a little neurotic..."[59]

---

[59] Freud, *SE* VI, 278.

Two

Finding Oneself in Heidegger's Early Philosophy

Anyone coming to Martin Heidegger's early philosophy for the first time faces a number of daunting challenges. For instance, Heidegger's notoriously impenetrable language can render his philosophical worldview difficult to grasp. In this chapter, we make minimal use of his "jargon"—although to some extent its inclusion is unavoidable—and stay, for the most part, with ordinary everyday English. For a variety of reasons, Heidegger's "new way of thinking" does not lend itself easily to clear and simple articulation. It is for these reasons we have chosen to approach Heidegger's early philosophy in an innovative way—from a third-person phenomenological perspective. That is, we invite readers to participate actively in a concrete way, by thinking about how they would respond to a situation in which they might find themselves. In this way, we hope to ease the readers' burden of understanding as clearly and simply as possible, the fundamentals of Heidegger's early philosophy.

DISCOVERING THE "WORLD"

Let us begin with a "thought scenario." Imagine you are Rene Descartes lying in your bed in the late morning (as is your habit) wondering about whether there is anything that you know to be true with certainty. It is as if you just "popped into existence." *What would you think?* All you are aware of is that you are "here" in some way. Initially, *upon reflection*, you at least seem to have *some* level of awareness of some kind of meaning about what you take to be some kind of reality. From this starting point you try to determine what you know to be true with certainty about reality. It is common knowledge that you (as Descartes) use methodical doubt to question the certainty of everything. After eliminating any dubious candidates, you arrive at one foundational, certain truth—the Cogito—*I think therefore I am.* Having established that, you now preoccupy yourself with the various *beings* you take to be real.[1] You then think that it makes sense to focus on the following kinds of questions: What types of fundamental beings are there? How many are there? What is the nature of each kind of being? What are its most basic properties? How do different kinds of beings interrelate?

---

[1] This is what Heidegger characterizes as "Thing-ontology." Heidegger, *Being and Time*, 133.

You might notice that this approach gets you to look at yourself as a kind of substance (thing or object). Furthermore, your trajectory of thinking makes you aware of other substances—for example, material or extended substances. This line of thinking gets you to view the world as exclusively composed of things or objects to be investigated. It may appear to be a viable way to begin your inquiry, but it inevitably leads you to approach self, world, and others from a specific perspective. Heidegger argues that it is this way of thinking that has egregiously dominated almost the entire Western philosophical tradition extending back to Plato and Aristotle. Perhaps there is an alternative way of looking at the world?

If instead, you were to turn back on yourself to question the *kinds* of questions you are raising and the way you have structured them up until now, your thinking might lead you in a different direction. After all, everything seems to hinge upon *what* questions you choose to ask and *how* you go about asking them. Could it be the case that you are asking the wrong questions, or structuring your questions in a way that might mislead you from the outset? Without being aware of it, is it possible that you have built-in, uncritically reflected upon presuppositions into the very structure and content of your questions? If so, this might take you down a road that could have disastrous implications for your contemporary theoretical orientations and in your everyday concrete practice. It is for this reason that Heidegger insists that *from the outset of our inquiry* we must be careful to work out the right questions to ask and formulate them in a way that is most appropriate to their subject matter.[2]

In other words, it might be viable to ask or structure questions in an alternative way than Descartes' that discloses what these other questions could not. How? Suppose you are at the point when you think you have just "popped into existence" but are open to a different way of thinking. You could, for example, simply focus on your sheer awareness that anything *is* at all. Here it is important to pause and notice that *when* you do this you always already have some level of understanding of what it means to be that you are using in your everyday existence, and yet this occurs on a level about which you do not *explicitly* think. You might go on to wonder: how is it possible *that* there is being (whatever it is)? What does it *mean* to *be,* anyway? From the outset, you are simply aware of a field of meaning. All you experience is this field of meaning and your awareness of it. (It turns out that they are one and the same.)

You wonder: What has *happened* here? What does it mean for me to *be?* Your very being is an issue for you—that you *are* matters to you. Now, you stand back and ask what must be the case (i.e., what must you presuppose) in order for it to be possible for you to think about and experience meaning at all? These are Heidegger's initial questions. They are the basic ones for what

---

[2] Ibid., 24; see also Heidegger, *Zollikon Seminars*, 259, 26-7; 33, 35, 37, 121, 222.

Heidegger calls *"fundamental ontology."*[3]   Upon reflection you see that they involve an entirely different way of thinking than the first mode described. They are ones that Heidegger contends have been *forgotten* by a tradition that exclusively preoccupies itself with things to be studied (e.g., Descartes' mode of approach).

It is these two different modes of inquiry that are separated by what Heidegger calls the "ontological difference."[4]   On the one hand, if you inquire into beings exclusively, you reduce everything into some sort of being (i.e., thing, object, or "thing-ontology") to be investigated. If you then inquire into human beings, you might develop theories regarding the *nature* of human beings (i.e., theories of human nature, or "philosophical anthropology"). On the other hand, if you focus on *what it means to be* as an awareness of being, you develop a genuine ontological inquiry. Heidegger claims that the former mode of inquiry loses (however unwittingly) our very humanity by distorting it from the outset (i.e., by making it into an object), while it is the latter mode that enables us to understand our existence on the deepest primordial level.

We now proceed to the second major facet of our thought scenario. If you choose to inquire into what it means to be as an awareness of being, what would be the best *method* to describe it? The simplest method would seem to be to *let be* that which shows itself as it shows itself (in other words, not to impose on that which shows itself any uncritically held presuppositions).[5] But where should you begin? It seems it would make sense to start with yourself since it is *you* who not only wonder about what it means to be (that is, the fact that you *are* is an issue for you—you are the one who has raised the question), but have some understanding (however implicit) of what it means to be. Hence, you are trying to let be shown what it means for you to *be*, in other words, to move from an implicit everyday understanding of what it means to be, to an explicit understanding.   In order to do this, you will need to uncover what must be presupposed and makes it possible for you to let be shown what it means to be. This is the method that Heidegger calls *"phenomenology."*

We now turn the third major characteristic of our thought scenario. In order to conduct your inquiry of letting be shown what it means for you to be, you see that you already find yourself in *some kind of set of circumstances*. And now it is *necessary* for you to make a fundamental departure from the original thought scenario—you did not really just "pop into existence" in the first place at all! You always *already* find yourself immersed within your world via your personal and practical concerns, that is, you always already exist within an individual and world historical flow of meaningful processes. This is one of the primary reasons a preoccupation with investigating things is *not* as primordial to your existence as this new form of inquiry—by doing the

---

[3] Heidegger, *Being and Time*, 31f; see also, Heidegger, *Zollikon Seminars*, 122, 203.
[4] Heidegger, *Zollikon Seminars*, 31, 192, 204.
[5] Heidegger, *Being and Time*, 49f, 58f; see also, Heidegger, *Zollikon Seminars*, 59, 64, 76, 110, 131-32; 197-98.

former, the *context* of your *relatedness* to beings has been severed. When you, as Descartes, conducted your inquiry into beings, it turns out that this presupposed that your everyday existence was already underway. That is, it occurs as part of your field of meaning which presupposes a historical flow in which you are always already immersed in your personal, practical, public, and theoretical concerns; you cannot, for example, "look at a thing" unless you already have some understanding of what is meant by "a thing." Take Descartes' life, for example. The development of his philosophy certainly did not occur in a vacuum, but in a rich historical context.

To get a sense of the contextual flavor of Descartes' everyday life let us consider a very brief account. His mother died when he was an infant, and his grandmother raised him. At a Jesuit college, he received a classical, scientific, and philosophical education, and subsequently earned a degree in Law. Philosophically, he rejected Aristotelian "natural science," and was powerfully influenced by the theoretical roads blazed by Galileo. After college, he joined the army, and nurtured a taste for gambling. He traveled widely, throughout Europe—particularly, Bavaria, the Netherlands, Italy, and so forth. Coming from a family heritage of medical doctors, at age 31 he conducted dissections on human organs to study anatomy. At the age of 39 he had an illegitimate daughter with a servant who died the year his book, *Meditations*, was published (as did his father and one of his sisters). He preferred to live in solitude (though always with servants). Emotionally, he favored the stoic acceptance of whatever happens. The point of this description is that Descartes too was always already immersed in his field of meaning in which his historical context serves as a necessary backdrop.[6]

To return to our thought scenario, one given fundamental aspect of these circumstances is that you are a being who always already finds yourself *interpreting* what you take to be a "world." That is, *interpretation* is a *way of your being* in the world. So you are concerned with the interpretation of the being (i.e., yourself) who is always already interpreting the world. Yet, this is precisely *one* of those fundamental characteristics that you wanted to *let be* shown. Indeed, to understand the basic conditions that make interpretation itself possible, we must *already be* interpreting beings through which those conditions themselves are invariably already operative. Your problem is that you *always already* find yourself smack-dab in a circle that is always already in process, that is, human existence is a circle. This is what Heidegger calls "the hermeneutical circle."[7] Hence, there is a built-in, reciprocal ontological relationship between the interpreter (i.e., you as the interpreting being, have,

---

[6] And one that serves as the soil from which his philosophy emerged, though we cannot develop this here.
[7] Heidegger, *Being and Time*, 195, 362-63; see also, Heidegger, *Zollikon Seminars*, 36-37, 27, 140.

on some level, some understanding of what it means to be) and the "text" (your everyday Being-in-the-world).[8]

Your question now is how to find a way to enter this circle in the right way. You also find that you always already exist and interpret in a larger flow of history—not just your individual self-history. You observe that there are others ostensibly following the very same process of interpreting the world. As such, concrete everyday human existence is the text to be interpreted, both individually *and* globally. This is the mode of inquiry that Heidegger describes as "hermeneutics."[9]

Thus, Heidegger's early philosophy can be described as *hermeneutical phenomenological ontology*. It endeavors to describe how it is possible—and what must be presupposed—for individuals to interpret what it means to be *as a way of being* within an overall historical flow and context, by *letting beings be* as they are, *as* they are disclosed by us. This, of course, is an enormously ambitious project. Heidegger is trying to show how *any* experience of reflection and *meaning* and/or significance *is possible at all*. This is the project Heidegger undertakes in *Being and Time*.

WHAT MUST BE PRESUPPOSED IN ORDER FOR IT TO BE POSSIBLE THAT I AM?

Now, how might you characterize this field of meaning in the most general way possible? Heidegger used the following figure to represent this field of meaning allegorically:[10]

Each circle or arrow represents what Heidegger describes as an individual "Dasein"—a being who is there *as* a "situatedness" of some kind—a field of meaning.

Heidegger discloses several fundamental characteristics of you as Dasein. First, you are that site of *openness* or clearing in which the "world" appears as a unified contextual whole field of meaning—your *Being-in-the-world*.[11] You *are* the openness in which you encounter beings as meaningful,

---

[8] Heidegger also emphasizes that our fundamental ontological way of being and our everyday existence are mutually rooted in one another. As such, the hermeneutical circle is intrinsic to the very structure of our finite, temporal, being-in-the-world.

[9] Heidegger, *Being and Time*, 62f.; see also, Heidegger, *Zollikon Seminars*, 120, 125, 223.

[10] Heidegger drew this on a chalkboard at the Burgholzli Psychiatric Hospital during his first Zollikon seminar for psychotherapists, psychoanalysts, psychiatrists, etc. in 1959. (Heidegger, *Zollikon Seminars*, 3.)

[11] Heidegger, *Being and Time*, 78f. This is what Heidegger characterizes as *Being-in-the-world* and *existence*, i.e., that which most fundamentally characterizes the *way of being* that you *are*.

and it is your own way of being as awareness that holds-open this field. This means that you find yourself as always already situated within such a unified field of meaning of *relatedness*. Furthermore, you are the *transitive* awareness of the fact that you are always *situated here* in a set of circumstances that are *in process*.

Another way to think of this "Being-in-the-world" is as *a clearing*[12] in which you encounter actualities and possibilities. That is, you notice that you are the being that shows whatever presents itself within it, and you disclose that it involves *actualities* and *possibilities*. There are given features that are intrinsic to your field of meaning to which you might relate in one way or another as you are immersed in your field of meaning. As such, they are all interrelated as part of a unified contextual whole. In other words, your Being-in-the-world (as a unified field of meaning) is your Being-one's-Self.[13] The crucial point is that this clearing is necessary for anything at all to appear, or to be absent. Without it, there could be no relatedness at all, no meaning, significance, and so forth.

Another important way for you to think of this site of openness, that you are as Dasein, is *as* the "Free." Here, you might limit your understanding of the free in terms of a "freedom to choose" from a number of options in the everyday existential and/or psychological sense, but this would be a mistake. To reduce our understanding of freedom in such a narrow way would be, Heidegger claims, to "surrender to the arbitrariness of this 'wavering reed' (i.e., human caprice)."[14] Alternatively, if you do not put unnecessary restrictions on your "freedom," upon reflection you might discover a deeper, more "original" and "primordial" notion of freedom. Since you freely enter into your openness, you *are* free to be *open* to whatever you encounter.[15] You have the capacity to encounter other beings (i.e., actualities) and potential ways of being (i.e., possibilities) in this open region (i.e., the world) precisely because you are free. As such, you can be more or less open to this mode of existence. The more you are open, the more freedom is disclosed; the less you are open, the more freedom becomes concealed from your life. It is an issue of the extent to which you allow yourself to be open, to participate within the

---

[12] Ibid., 214, 401; also see, Heidegger, *Zollikon Seminars*, 159, 178, 180, 206, 281. For a more complete discussion of this involved notion see Askay and Farquhar, *Apprehending the Inaccessible*, 205-10.
[13] Heidegger, *Being and Time*, 65, 318; also see, Heidegger, *Zollikon Seminars*, 174.
[14] Heidegger, *Basic Writings*, 126. Heidegger rejects the notion of freedom that we counter-pose to "determinism" as a-causal *as the most primordial notion of freedom*. And yet, he points out, it is the one that unfortunately dominates our contemporary philosophical and everyday cultural milieu.
[15] This is Heidegger's crucial ontological conception of freedom. Heidegger, *Being and Time,* 331; Heidegger, *Basic Writings,* 127-32; Heidegger, *Zollikon Seminars*, 14n., 15, 217; Martin Heidegger, *Parmenides*, trans. André Schuwer and Richard Rojcewicz (Bloomington: Indiana University Press, 1992), 149.

openness. On the one hand, you can be freed from constrictive possibilities.[16] On the other, you can be "freed to" expand your possibilities, to think and *be* in new ways.

It is also important to note the intimate relationship that exists between "freedom" and *letting be* for Heidegger: "Freedom for what is opened up in an open region *lets beings be* the beings they are."[17] It is this ontological capacity for freedom that makes it possible for Dasein to let beings be, i.e., show themselves *as* they are in themselves. This letting-be has a dual aspect. Dasein both receives and perceives beings simultaneously.[18] In both, Dasein discloses something that was in a sense *hidden* before encountering it. On the one hand, you are actively engaged in any situation in which you find yourself by being concernfully involved, that is, it matters to you in some way. *As* this capacity, in a sense, you interrogate it in the way you might interrogate a witness in court to find out some truth. On the other hand, it is as though you "step back" into the open region and become a presence which permits all presences to show themselves, a witness to what occurs, that is, you receive it; you take-in or listen-in on what *presences* itself. It is this *capacity to receive-perceive* the *significance* of what is encountered that constitutes Dasein's whole *way of being*.[19] Without this capacity you would not experience the world as significant or meaningful in any way.

Furthermore, as the clearing, Dasein is simultaneously involved in a field of meaning that is disclosed *and* concealed. Another way of saying this is that we exist in the truth and the untruth at the same time. The "truth" of being might show itself in letting beings be what they are, yet also hide itself. That which is *as* it presences itself to us has hidden dimensions (some of which remain hidden) *as* we disclose its meaning.[20] The clearing—as a field of disclosedness—is also a field of hiddenness.

It is now important to return to Heidegger's illustration above. His drawing has several other features that are important to note. First, it illustrates Dasein's intrinsic *incompleteness*. We are never complete in our existence until we die; we are always *in process*. There is a certain *open-endedness* to existence in terms of our possibilities—they seem to involve an unlimited number of directions we are able to pursue in life. Second, *finitude* is intrinsic to our situatedness as well. This is manifested in various ways. For example, by making a choice and acting upon it, we necessarily preclude

---

[16] Heidegger, *Zollikon Seminars*, 134.

[17] Heidegger, *Basic Writings*, 127; see also, Heidegger, *Being and time*, 117f.; Heidegger, *Zollikon Seminars*, 223-24.

[18] The German word "Vernehmen" has this double sense here. See Heidegger, *Zollikon Seminars*, 132n.

[19] Heidegger, *Zollikon Seminars*, 231.

[20] This fact that that which is hidden manifests itself at all is what Heidegger dubbed "the mystery." Ibid., 183.

the possibility of other choices and actions.[21] Our existence is also limited by whatever the duration is between birth and death.

Next, there is a reason that Heidegger drew several circles in his illustration. By doing so, he is representing the idea that you are not the only being in the world that exists as a clearing—that is, there are other Daseins. This fact forms an intrinsic aspect of the givenness of your situation. However, we shall take up this vital point more extensively later.

To continue, we should be careful to note that each of the circles represents that each of the group of Daseins has a certain *"mineness"* in existence. It is each Dasein's own unique and irreplaceable existence that one experiences in his or her own individuality. You *are* you (or at least you think you are).

Finally, you simply find yourself "thrown" *as* this clearing. In light of our thought scenario, you simply find yourself "here" amidst these givens (i.e., actualities). You did not choose for them to be here, but rather they are simply given aspects of the way reality *is* as you relate to it. The openness itself is "there" regardless of any human choice. Freedom is not simply free-floating but engages a "facticity:" all those aspects of the human condition that are simply given, and not chosen.[22] This is what Heidegger calls our "thrownness."[23] For example, the fact that you are *as* a site of openness at all is a given, and not something chosen. It cannot be "escaped;" it can only be concealed. This givenness is an intrinsic aspect of the human condition.

Another element of facticity is that our *existential* capacity to choose is itself a given. Hence, this primordial sense of freedom (as openness) makes possible all other levels of freedom (e.g., "existential freedom,"[24] psychological freedom, and so forth). You can only be free in your existential "freedom of choice" because you are primordially exposed to the free and open dimension (i.e., clearing) of being in the first place.[25] Hence, your existence itself is a free *way* of being. By being a disclosedness of your own possibilities, you are set free for various ways of being yourself.

There is at least one major characteristic of our existence that Heidegger's illustration is not able to capture. It involves *how* you are *as* this site of openness. You understand yourself as a dynamic *process* that is always in the process of *happening* as you go about coping with your existence. As such, you *are* your possibilities. You are not a fixed "thing" or "object" with static properties. This is, of course, crucial to Heidegger's point that Dasein is not a being (i.e., a thing of some kind) to be investigated, but rather a being to be understood *as* one understands oneself.

---

[21] Heidegger, *Being and Time*, 331.
[22] Ibid., 82; see also, Heidegger, *Zollikon Seminars*, 139.
[23] Heidegger, *Being and Time*, 174.
[24] Ibid., 232.
[25] Ibid., 331; see also, Heidegger, *Basic Writings*, 125.

WHAT MAKES IT POSSIBLE TO RELATE TO THE MOST BASIC KINDS OF BEINGS?

Let us return to our original thought scenario. You know that you are here as an openness and that one major aspect of this openness is that you are *as* a field of meaning or relatedness. The natural question is: to *what* or *whom* do you relate within this field? Upon reflection you realize that you relate most generally to what you take to be the physical environment, other beings like you, and yourself.[26] To say you relate is also to say you disclose whom or what you encounter. It seems natural now to *ask, how it is possible* for us to relate to each of these? Another way of asking this question is: what fundamental structures of human existence are presupposed and make it possible for us to experience any meaning whatsoever (as these are disclosed to us, by us, in our own process of existing).[27]

You might notice how you most proximally and originally exist in your everyday "world." First, it is not possible to imagine yourself without a world to which you are already in relation. Also, you always already *dwell* in a world with which you are familiar. As such, you find yourself concernfully *involved* in this world in a multiplicity of interrelated projects and activities—coping, disclosing, investigating, understanding, producing, and so forth. It is in terms of these concerns that things take on the meaning or significance they have for you. "World," then, is the field of meaning in which you are involved. *It is your very context*—your Being-in-the-world. As such, it provides the a priori ground for your very possibility of feeling at home.

Now you might ask, what is necessary in order for me to be in "the-world" (i.e., what are the fundamental structures which make it possible for me to have a world)? How do I relate to my natural and human-made environment most typically in my everyday existence? If you are careful, you will notice that you most typically use your environment without reflecting upon it. When, for example, you use tools, you do not apprehend them thematically as particular objects. Instead, you are immersed in the concrete *process* of using them as you go about accomplishing projects within a complex network of meanings in your everyday life.[28] It is, of course, possible for you to assume a theoretical stance (e.g., as in scientific inquiry) toward nature or human-made objects and see them as objects to be investigated, or you might turn and reflect upon the tool you are using as an object if it breaks down or is missing and is no longer usable. But these are not the most primordial ways in which you relate to them.

---

[26] Heidegger, *Zollikon Seminars*, 144, 159. Heidegger's word for such relatedness is "sojourning."

[27] In *Being and Time,* Heidegger calls this "the existential analytic"—the mapping out of the fundamental structures intrinsic to Dasein's way of Being. (pp. 67ff.)

[28] This act of using is a way of our Being Heidegger calls "readiness-to hand." Ibid., 98.

As you are "here" in your field of meaning, you notice that you are always already exercising your capacity to relate to other persons in some way.[29] For example, you might be cooperating with others on some kind of project that involves shared concerns, you might seek to avoid others by escaping to a cabin in the woods, and so forth. Others thus form an intrinsic dimension of everyday existence. An aspect of your very way of being is as a relatedness to other persons. Heidegger calls this "Being-with."[30] It is the ontological structure that is presupposed and makes it possible for us to relate to other Daseins in any way whatsoever within our shared field of meaning. We share an overlapping world in our openness to whatever we encounter together.[31] In addition, we meet others in their field of meaning as beings who also have their own practical and personal concerns and projects, and as a complex network of relationships with others. Others, then, play a central role in any individual's field of meaning; the individual can never be truly understood as isolated.

It is also possible, of course, for you to disclose the other as part of your personal concern. It is our common structure as Being-with which enables this to occur—making possible a way of our Being together understandingly, or with *empathy*. Making Daseins mutually transparent is possible only since Dasein, as Being-in-the-world, is always already with others. It is not, then, some "psychical capacity" between psychological subjects that enables us to relate understandingly to one another,[32] rather Being-with makes the empathic relatedeness between individuals possible.

This brings us to the importance of *listening-in* for Heidegger: "Listening to...is Dasein's way of Being-open as Being-with...hearing constitutes the primary way in which Dasein is open...Dasein hears, because it understands."[33] For Heidegger, listening/hearing is the primary mode of Dasein's being open as Being-with which makes it possible to understand our possibilities in our relations with ourselves and others. It is because human beings exist as always already immersed in a quotidian life of concerns *first* that hearing a sound can take on any meaning whatsoever.[34] This is what Heidegger means when he says, "Only he who already understands can listen."[35] Furthermore, it is our "Understanding" as an ontological structure that is presupposed and makes it possible for us to listen-to another Dasein, and for it to have meaning/significance.

---

[29] Ibid., 149-63; Heidegger, *The Basic Problems of Phenomenology*, 297; Heidegger, *Zollikon Seminars*, 111.

[30] Heidegger, *Being and Time*, 158.

[31] This is one of the primary ways that Heidegger's illustration of the several sites of openness (as individuals) breaks down in relation to his own position. The individual circles must overlap since our everyday concerns intersect those of others.

[32] Ibid., 162-63.

[33] Ibid., 206.

[34] Heidegger, *History of the Concept of Time*, 266.

[35] Heidegger, *Being and Time*, 207.

Having seen what must be presupposed and makes it possible to relate to nature, everyday objects, and others, we are now ready to consider how we most primordially *relate to ourselves* in our everyday lives.

WHAT IS THE MOST BASIC WAY I RELATE TO MYSELF IN EVERYDAY LIFE?

At one time or another, each one of us has asked ourselves a basic question, "Who am I?" In response, we assume that we have reflected upon life, made decisions, and lived our lives in a way that made sense. It is here that Heidegger makes a striking observation: *You may very well not be who you take yourself to be.* What could this possibly mean?

To return to our thought scenario, it might occur to you that the "here" into which you have been thrown has a given meaning that has already been constructed for you simply to adopt and to interpret your world (including yourself) in terms of this prefabricated construction. But constructed by whom? For what purpose?

In everyday life *we typically take ourselves to be* beings that freely do our own thinking, make our own decisions, and act in the world in the way that we (*as individuals*) think is the proper way to behave. Heidegger's contention is that, for most people most of the time, *this simply is not true.* Instead, he claims, we are most typically in a mode in which our thoughts, our interpretations have already been pre-packaged for us, and we simply take over the way in which a public mentality has already interpreted the world. This is what Heidegger calls the "they-self" mode.[36] The point is that the *who* that we have taken ourselves to be is really nothing more than the *who* of this anonymous public way (an "anonymous One") of interpreting the world.[37] Dasein loses its self-awareness of its own possibilities, and becomes absorbed into the world of objects, for example; it becomes preoccupied with its practical everyday concerns. Heidegger describes this mode of existing as "falleness" and "inauthenticity."[38] People lose self-awareness of their possibilities; they permit their capacities for choice making to lie dormant, and adopt the mode of "public awareness," all the while believing that they are leading the fullest and most genuine lives.

While doing so we tend to adopt various kinds of evasive tactics. For example, we preoccupy ourselves with superficial talk or gossip about relatively trivial aspects of everyday existence. This is a form of what Heidegger calls "idle talk." Or, we might simply allow ourselves to be in a mode of curiosity for curiosity's sake so that we avoid truly genuine concerns. We might also allow ourselves to be absorbed in a sphere of everyday life that

---

[36] Ibid., 167, 210.
[37] Ibid., 163ff.
[38] Ibid., 219ff; see also, Heidegger, *History of the Concept of Time*, 272ff.; Heidegger, *Zollikon Seminars*, 137, 174, 205.

is so nebulous, that we subject ourselves to a barrage of potentially endless possible interpretations, never settling down on any one in any substantive way.[39] By not having to choose, and accept the concomitant responsibility, Dasein exists as *tranquil*. At the same time it exists as *alienating* because it exists as diverted from its own self-chosen possibilities, that is, from being a genuine self.

Interestingly, Heidegger insists that the "they-self" mode of self is the most primordial.[40] When we are born into a world, we are essentially "thrown" into a world of meaning and interpretations that have already been assigned in a global and public way. For the early part of our lives, the "they" perspective *pervasively* forms the essential background through which we make sense of the world in our everyday practice. At this juncture, we have no alternative. We would not be able to cope in the world without them (e.g., generally, "red lights or signs" mean stop, cars must be driven on the right side of the road in the US, it is a bad idea to use the freeway as a playground, etc.). The pervasiveness of such interpretations extends across the *entire* spectrum of personal, public, practical, and theoretical concerns.

Some individuals may spend their entire lives in this "they-self" mode. They may be utterly content with simply "going with the flow" of that way of interpreting the world that has been pre-interpreted for them. What matters to them, is what matters to the "they;" how they understand the world is how this public way of interpreting the world understands it, and they are absorbed in the world in such as way that they are concerned with the trivialities and superficialities with which the "they-self" concerns itself. To lose their "they-self" mode would be a terrifying possibility for such people.

One important manifestation of the "they-self" mode of existence is that we are in both the *truth and untruth* simultaneously. On the one hand, its way of interpreting may involve givens which *just are;* for example, the fact that when we choose to act on one possibility, we thereby exclude others. On the other hand, the problem is that this pre-formulated way of interpreting the world may intrude into your existence in ways you find confining and unacceptable. It may extend to areas of your life in which you think it has no proper place. It may tell you what it takes the "proper moral sphere" to be, what the "appropriate source" of knowledge is, within what spectrum your religious beliefs ought to fall, how you should think and speak about the place of death in your life, from what categories of political affiliation you *must* select, and so forth.

In the face of these interpretations (as givens), there comes a time for each of us when we must face a choice: simply "go with the flow" and let this anonymous, public way of interpreting make sense of the world for us and act

---

[39] For an extended discussion of these tactics which comprise what Heidegger calls modes of "fallenness" see Heidegger, *Being and Time*, 211-18; Heidegger, *History of the Concept of Time,* 272-80.

[40] Heidegger, *Being and Time*, 168.

accordingly, or take hold of our own possibilities and reflect upon our options, act upon our choices (else they mean nothing), and assume our rightful responsibility for what happens. Our option then is to become authentically ourselves, or not.

To illustrate graphically what Heidegger has in mind, let us return to the narrative of our thought scenario. At this point, we might think to ourselves, it all seems so *simple*, that is, we *are* those beings that *freely open* up the *meaning* of whatever beings we encounter *as we relate* to them.[41] What could be clearer? This brings us to one of the greatest ironies of our existence, according to Heidegger. It is that which is nearest, simplest, and most familiar to us that is not easily accessible and yet is *most important* to us:[42] the very being-open of our own field of meaning. We are *so close* to this *field* on the everyday level *as we live it,* that we remain *oblivious* to our own specific state of being-open, that is, a deeper understanding of what it means to be.[43]

Why does this happen? Heidegger suggests that the reason we are oblivious to our simply being-open to being is because of the human tendency to fall prey to the mode of thinking (i.e., one variant of the "they-self" mode) we described at the inception of our discussion. One primary example of this today is what we might recognize as the unreflective adoption of "scientific thinking" as *the* exclusionary perspective leading to genuine truth. Heidegger held that, to the contrary, this worldview has blinded us from apprehending this fundamental aspect of our existence.[44] So, instead of letting beings be (or show themselves as they are), our tendency is to *impose* complex interpretive models upon beings (which includes the presumption that it is only beings that are worthy of investigation in the first place), and require those beings to conform to our model. So, for example, we "continuously overlook [our being-open] in favor of contrived psychological theories."[45] The result is that the letting-be of the human being in light of Dasein is extremely difficult, unfamiliar."[46] For Heidegger, this is nothing short of disastrous—it is to forget the *wonder* that we *are* at all.

---

[41] Indeed, this is what Heidegger refers to as "the simple." Heidegger, *Zollikon Seminars,* 102, 263.
[42] It is fascinating to note that Ludwig Wittgenstein—another great German philosopher of the twentieth century—made precisely the same point in his magnum opus, *Philosophical Investigations.* (Ludwig Wittgenstein, *Philosophical Investigations*, trans. Gertrude Elizabeth Anscombe (New York: Macmillan Company, 1971), 129, 50.
[43] Heidegger, *Being and Time*, 36-37; 69, 119.
[44] Heidegger, *Zollikon Seminars*, 102. Heidegger calls this "calculative thinking." Ibid., 112, 263.
[45] Ibid., 74; see also, Heidegger, *Being and Time*, 69.
[46] Heidegger, *Zollikon Seminars*, 223; see also, Heidegger, *Being and Time*, 423.

WHAT MUST BE PRESUPPOSED IN ORDER FOR THE ACTUALITIES AND POSSIBILITIES OF MY EXISTENCE TO BE POSSIBLE?

Continuing again with our narrative, we have seen that in our openness as a field of meaning that we *disclose*, there are *actualities* (given aspects of our situation that we have not chosen) and *possibilities* (from among which we may select as options). We might now ask: What fundamental structures must be presupposed and *make it possible* for us to encounter (disclose) our actualities and to be (disclose) our possibilities *as* our field of meaning?

Let us begin with our capacity to encounter actualities. In any situation (or clearing), we always already *find* ourselves "attuned" to our relatedness to self, others, and environment at a certain "pitch."[47] In our original thought scenario, you notice that you are attuned to your being "here" in a variety of possible ways. You may be curious about it, angry, shocked, surprised, and so forth. Heidegger calls these "modes of attunement." "Attunements are the fundamental ways in which we find ourselves."[48] They are the "how" in the question, "How do you find yourself today?"—or more colloquially, "How are you?" Heidegger uses the German word "Befindlichkeit" for this mode of being which literally refers to how one finds oneself within ones current life experience.[49] The dominant mode of attunement at any given time serves as the condition of our openness for perceiving and dealing with what we encounter. If you are joyful, for example, your entire Being-in-the-world is lit up by this joyfulness. Also, "attunement is…the way of our being there with one another."[50] It is the way in which we find ourselves attuned to one another. Attunements serve as the "medium" through which things happen,[51] and are what enable the *given* actualities in our world (e.g., things/other people, etc.) to *matter* to us in the way they do. For Heidegger, they disclose to us our "facticity" and "thrownness." These modes of attunement are not freely chosen, but "descend upon us."[52] This is not to say that we must simply endure being them. Heidegger insists that a person "can, should and must, through knowledge and will, become master" of them.[53] They provide an ideal opportunity to disclose who we are as individual Dasein, as well as our shared being-in-the-world.

Not all modes of attunement are equally important in terms of their capacity to disclose our world to us. For example, resentment, jealousy, fear, anger, hatred, and so forth, are relatively *transitory* feelings and tend to focus

---

[47] Heidegger, *Zollikon Seminars*, 165, 203, 206; Heidegger, *Being and Time*, 176.
[48] Martin Heidegger, *The Fundamental Concepts of Metaphysics: World, Finitude, Solitude*, trans. William McNeill and Nicholas Walker (Bloomington: Indiana University Press, 1995), 67.
[49] Heidegger, *Being and Time*, 172.
[50] Heidegger, *The Fundamental Concepts of Metaphysics*, 66.
[51] Ibid., 68.
[52] Heidegger, *Being and Time*, 136.
[53] Ibid., 175; see also, Heidegger, *Zollikon Seminars*, 166.

on *particular* aspects of our world. In contrast, there are modes of attunement that are more fundamental than such fleeting and localized feelings,[54] modes in which one always finds oneself attuned to one's *whole* set of circumstances in some way.[55] Heidegger points out that we can slip into these modes without being aware of it—such fundamental attunements are "slumbering."[56] When this occurs, the most powerful modes of attunement can typically manifest a condition in which we are fleeing from some being or recognition.   Since these fundamental modes of attunement draw our attention to the whole of our existence they can lead us back into primordial aspects of the human condition that remain hidden from us.[57] Hence, Heidegger insists, we must "let them be" awakened.[58] For, such modes are maximally disclosive of our existence. Heidegger thinks that it is to these that we ought to devote our attention.

What specifically are these fundamental modes of attunement that Heidegger has in mind that light up the whole situation in which we find ourselves? They are: "Angst" (existential anxiety), "profound boredom," and "joy." Heidegger did not provide an extensive analysis of joy in this respect.[59] He did, however, recognize the need for an exhaustive analysis of Angst[60] and of "profound boredom."[61] We shall focus on Angst in the subsequent section since it is pivotal to the way we are attuned to the context in which we find ourselves.

Attunement, according to Heidegger, is always in relationship to our *Understanding*—the second fundamental ontological structure that discloses our Being-in-the-world.[62] Understanding makes it possible for us to become aware of our *possibilities*. It makes it possible for us to be able-to-be, act in the world, and find our way in it. Furthermore, it is intrinsic to our *way of Being* so that we can move forward into the future, or be aware of and press into the possibilities we encounter. Heidegger calls our Understanding, as an existential structure, "projection."[63]   It is because of our projection of possibilities that we come to understand things and others. It makes it possible for us to throw ourselves into our possibilities and to disclose others in their own possibilities as we project possibilities for ourselves.[64]

---

[54] Heidegger, *Being and Time*, 136, 175.
[55] Ibid., 176.
[56] Heidegger, *The Fundamental Concepts of Metaphysics*, 59, 61, 65.
[57] Ibid., 68.
[58] Ibid., 59, 61, 65.
[59] Heidegger, *Zollikon Seminars*, 166; Heidegger, *Being and Time*, 173, 358; Heidegger, *Basic Writings*, 101; see also, Boss, *Existential Foundations in Medicine and Psychology*, 112.
[60] Heidegger, *Zollikon Seminars*, 62, 143; Heidegger, *Being and Time*, 228-35, 309-11, 321f, 342f, 392f.; Heidegger, *Basic Writings*, 102f.
[61] Heidegger, *The Fundamental Concepts of Metaphysics*, 78-169.
[62] Heidegger, *Being and Time*, 182-202.
[63] Ibid., 185.
[64] Ibid., 184.

We should also note that we find ourselves in the world always already as *thrown possibility*. It is part of our *given way of being* to be/have possibilities—definite possibilities, past possibilities, waived possibilities, seized possibilities, and so forth. In fact, we disclose other beings by letting them be involved in a possibility of our Being.[65] In this way they can take on a *significance* and be understood by us. Hence, it is clear that our *modes of attunement* are indissolubly related to our *understanding*; we can never have one without the other. This is the basis for our understanding of ourselves and the world as an *interplay* between the world as it *is* in its facticity (a given world and structure of human existence), and oneself as being possibilities and freedom.

It should be clear that for Heidegger we most concretely exist in our everyday lives as a field of meaning that is *in process* on a *pre-cognitive* level of awareness. We are always already immersed in our world in a more basic way than any cognitions and knowledge we might have of it.[66] On this level of pre-cognitive existential involvement, the mere act of apprehending a thing *as* a thing (e.g., as a house) always already involves the structure of *interpretation*. Whatever we encounter gets related to the holistic understanding that we already possess. We have already assigned it a place within the relational network of meaning that is our world. "Interpretation" is the "working out" of the possibilities projected by the understanding. It makes explicit that about which we are only implicitly aware in our experience. It always involves unpacking the presuppositions that underlie our apprehending some being that is presented to us.[67]

We are now in a position to answer one of our most fundamental questions: What is *meaning*? It is the *context of interrelatedness*—which originates from our capacity to project possibilities—in which a being (e.g., a person) is embedded; we are the disclosedness of the context of interrelatedness. It is because of this context that something gets understood in terms of its purpose or use and thereby becomes intelligible.

We have seen that on the most basic level we exist as an interplay of actualities and possibilities which we disclose. It may now occur to us to wonder whether there is a unifying structure presupposed by all of the other fundamental structures we have discussed so far. It seems that they must have something in common that provides a foundation for their interrelatedness. This structure Heidegger calls "Care." We as Dasein *are* care.[68] Anything one ever does manifests a mode of caring. This is because our very *way* of being is such that beings matter or are of concern to us. We care about our actualities, possibilities, and everyday absorbed involvements in the world. To exist is to care about who we are and our place in the world (on some level).

---

[65] Ibid., 116.
[66] Ibid., 190.
[67] Ibid., 191.
[68] Ibid., 235-41.

Now, it also may occur to us that there must be something that more primorially grounds and makes possible our Care in order for it to be *as a unity*.

What makes it possible for us to be as unified and caring sites of openness *as* fields of meaning is the fact that we are *temporal* beings.[69] Our experiences are meaningful to us because our very way of being is to be *as* a temporalizing process. What does this mean? We note that in any situation in which we find ourselves we are able to reflect upon it. What does it mean to "reflect"? It involves our capacity to "standout"[70] and think about what is going on.[71] It is because our *way of being* includes an awareness of our situation as necessarily involving actualities which already have been (past), and currently *are* (present), as well as potentially possible (future), that we might ask: how is this possible? Heidegger insists that it is essentially because our very *way of being* is to be processes intrinsically grounded by temporality. For example, in order to *be-possibilities*, presupposes that our very way of being is to be throwing ourselves forward into the *future*.[72] Indeed, it is because our way of being is temporality that we are able to anticipate our future possibilities, remember and reinterpret our past actions, and unify these in the present set of circumstances. Hence, to be, is to be *as* time.[73] Temporality is the origin of meaning or significance for our Being-in-the-world *as* a unity.

THE QUEST FOR AUTHENTIC EXISTENCE

We have seen that we find ourselves as always already thrown into "givens" into an open clearing as possibilities with temporality as its basis. Now *what are we to do*?

It is owing to the intrinsic way of being that we are as Dasein that we cannot avoid coming to some kind of basic decision about the being we are *as we are* (even if this occurs only on an implicit level in our everyday life). Each of us has already been involved in the question of existence from near the beginning of our lives (as we did in our original thought scenario). We have wondered generally "why" existence even occurs, or, given that it does, why should I exist? (What is the point of my existence?) As we reflect upon these "big" questions, and make decisions about them, we find that we are either thrown into our possibilities or have chosen them (or both). In any event, we find that we have no choice but to *take some sort of stand* concerning our existence. Do we resolutely take hold of our possibilities, and actively and honestly take part in the creation of our own world of meaning?

---

[69] Ibid., 277, 375; Heidegger, *Zollikon Seminars*, 38.

[70] This is taken from the ancient Greek word "ek-sist".

[71] Heidegger, *Being and Time*, 377; Heidegger, *Zollikon Seminars*, 121.

[72] Heidegger, *Being and Time*, 237.

[73] Ibid., 277, 375; Heidegger, *Zollikon Seminars*, 96.

Or do we flee from them? Or simply drift along in them, passively going with the flow of everyday existence? The first is what it means to be an authentic self; the second two characterize inauthentic existence. Here one might ask: If I choose to be the former, how do I go about doing so?

Heidegger observes that there will come a time when *some* individuals will stand-back and question the entire "they-self" interpretation of their existence. Why does this happen? Recall the pivotal idea that there are certain fundamental modes of attunement that descend on us and disclose the crucial features of the human condition as a whole—a disclosedness that up until then had remained hidden. "Angst" is one of those fundamental modes. It calls the entire context of our very being into question.

To see what this means, let us return to our thought scenario. Suppose your life seems to you to be proceeding smoothly, and you consider yourself to be relatively comfortable in the world. One day, you wake up and wonder to yourself, "Why?" "Does this world have any cosmic meaning or purpose?" "If not, why do I continue to live in it?" "What is the point of living?" "Why *be* at all?" You find these to be unsettling questions. What has happened? You find yourself in "Angst," or "existential anxiety."

In Angst, your very existence is shattered by a profound *existential* crisis of meaning. The meaning/significance of the world that you have taken for granted seems to have completely drained out of it. The entire world takes on the quality of "not-mattering" or insignificance.[74] "All things and we ourselves sink into indifference."[75] All beings, all meaning seems irrelevant and inconsequential. You experience a "naked strangeness" in the face of the world, and become "dazed by it."[76] You no longer feel at home with yourself in relation to the whole of existence.[77] Heidegger observes "Anxiety in the face of be-ing has never been greater than today."[78] You might wonder: during what kinds of situations does Angst arise? Heidegger suggests that it can occur at any time in even the most innocuous of situations.[79] As a mode of attunement, it does not require some sort of precipitating event or situation.[80] It simply happens! This is part of what makes it appear to be so elusive and mysterious from an everyday scientific perspective.

One primary aspect of this experience of "Angst" is that the "they-self" way of interpreting the world one has relied upon so heavily as the grounding for one's understanding of it, now has the "rug pulled out from under it"—"Everyday familiarity collapses."[81] It no longer serves its purpose

---

[74] Heidegger, *Being and Time*, 186, 231, 393.
[75] Heidegger, *Basic Writings*, 103.
[76] Heidegger, *Being and Time*, 394.
[77] Heidegger, *The Fundamental Concepts of Metaphysics*, 5.
[78] Martin Heidegger, *Contributions to Philosophy (From Enowning),* trans. Parvis Emad and Kenneth Maly (Bloomington: Indiana University Press, 1999), 97.
[79] Heidegger, *Being and Time*, 233-34; Heidegger, *History of the Concept of Time*, 289.
[80] Heidegger, *Basic Writings*, 108.
[81] Heidegger, *Being and Time*, 233.

of providing and expecting conformity to its arrogated interpretation of the world.[82] As a result, one feels distraught, alone, and adrift without a compass. One feels directionless. One feels like she or he has been plucked out of the flow of comfortable everyday existence and has fallen into an abyss whence there is no escape. One's very Being *as an issue* is brought into direct awareness once she or he no longer uncritically adopts the edifice of meaning constructed by the "they-self"—there no longer seems to be any point to existence. This is bad enough, but the situation gets even worse.

In genuine Angst, Dasein discovers that not only does the "they-self" not provide the foundation for existence, but *nothing else does either* (i.e., there is no cosmic meaningfulness or significance which underlies and sustains existence).[83] Angst discloses to us "the nothingness which forms the core of human existence."[84] It shows that, at bottom, we are nothing more than nothingness, that our existence is ultimately groundless, an abyss.[85] Dasein realizes that *even it* cannot provide the foundation or basis to its own being, and yet one must continue to cope with this given fact as long as one exists. This is part of what Heidegger calls the very "burden of our existence," and it is a primary aspect of what Heidegger refers to as *Being-guilty*.[86] All of us are "guilty" insofar as we have lived our lives as though there is a purpose, when, in actuality, existence has no deep meaning to ground it.

According to Heidegger, this is *the pivotal juncture* for one's existence. The individual has essentially four options. (1) One could give in to the lack of basis (i.e., the abyss) to one's existence, and commit suicide; (2) One could flee back into the comfort of the "they-self" interpretation, and once again lose or busy oneself in the flow of everyday existence;[87] (3) One could adopt an attitude that all actions are equally valid since there is no objective meaning, and do *anything* without any constraints; (4) Or one could authentically face up to the abyss, truly take hold of one's own possibilities, and act as one's own architect for this field of meaning.[88]

For Heidegger, option (2) and (3) both lead to an inauthentic existence. By becoming absorbed in the "they-self" mode, one "falls" into inauthenticity. Similarly, if one reduces all choice or activity to an equally meaningless endeavor, she or he has in essence embraced a *nihilistic* perspective on life—confirming the "they-self" in one's ultimate rejection.

---

[82] Heidegger, *Zollikon Seminars*, 187.

[83] Heidegger, *Being and Time*, 330.

[84] Ibid., 231-32; see also, Heidegger, *Basic Writings*, 93.

[85] Heidegger, *History of the Concept of Time*, 291.

[86] Heidegger, *Being and time*, 326f. It is important to understand that Heidegger's notion of guilt is not an ethico-moral concept. Instead, as an ontological structure, guilt provides the foundation for the very possibility of moral concepts and behavior. Ibid., 329.

[87] Ibid., 234; Heidegger, *History of the Concept of Time*, 293.

[88] Heidegger, *Being and Time*, 235.

Heidegger vociferously rejects this alternative.[89] He notes that one of the primary factors that lead to nihilism is the attitude and comportment toward *beings*, which, as we recall, was precisely our problem from the outset of our thought scenario. To comport ourselves exclusively toward beings is to lead us ultimately to the recognition of an objectively purposeless universe. The universe as a whole seems to have no point. However, unable to face this: "One refuses to admit the goal-lessness…[that this is] *the greatest nihilism* is precisely where one believes to have goals again, to be 'happy,' to attend to making equally available the 'cultural values' (movies and seaside resort vacations) to all the 'people'…[this] avoids a sheer desperation which simply cannot yet close its eyes to total meaninglessness."[90] Hence, nihilism itself tries to cover up the lack of deep meaning to our existence by simply contriving other "they-self" goals.

It is only in option 4—by actually taking hold of our own most possibilities—that we become truly who we are as authentic Dasein. This is what Heidegger means when he says that in the face of *our burden of existence*, "the self exists for the sake of its own self."[91] The individual has the opportunity to become aware that she or he must be the origin of meaning, to create one's own meaning/significance, and yet not fall prey to the illusion that this resoluteness provides a secure foundation for existence. This is "authentic existence"—when an individual is genuinely willing to reflect carefully, make choices based on one's reflections, act upon those choices (else they mean nothing), and assume responsibility for the consequences that ensue.

But how exactly does one make this transition from inauthentic to authentic existence? First one must settle down and be silent in order to hear what Heidegger refers to as "the call of conscience." It is the call from the genuine self to be no longer in the "they-self" mode (i.e., an inauthentic way of interpreting the world).[92] It is in understanding the "call" that Dasein has chosen itself as an authentic self, as "wanting to have a conscience."[93] The intention of the call from the genuine self is to get us to take hold of our possibilities and interpret the world as we freely choose within our field of meaning, being honest about whatever the givens are, and being accountable for our choices and actions.[94]

At this point, the "they-self" reacts to protect itself and will make a *cunning* move—even though it may not be aware of doing so. It will often conflate genuine "Angst" with "fear." For Heidegger, there is an important distinction between the two. Angst is always *global* whereas fear is always

---

[89] Heidegger, *Contributions to Philosophy,* 96ff.; Heidegger, *Zollikon Seminars*, 32-34, 136-44, 224, 262.
[90] Heidegger, *Contributions to Philosophy*, 97-98.
[91] Heidegger, *The Basic Problems of Phenomenology*, 170.
[92] Heidegger, *Being and Time*, 207f.; Heidegger, *Zollikon Seminars*, 97.
[93] Heidegger, *Being and Time*, 334.
[94] Ibid., 313f, 334f.

about some *particular* kind of being or event that is perceived as a threat.[95] One problem is that, for example, the psychological community as institutional representatives of the "they-self" fails to (or does not want to) recognize "Angst" as a fundamental mode of attunement, and reduces all forms of anxiety to modes of fear—an *everyday* mode of attunement. The result is that genuine Angst gets concealed and dealt with as fear, and whatever else Angst discloses gets covered-up as well. This is disastrous according to Heidegger, since one of the primary routes to the achievement of authentic existence is thereby closed-off.

Once Dasein has experienced Angst and its disclosure of this burden of existence, it is possible for another fundamental mode of attunement to ameliorate it—that of joy.[96] Dasein realizes that it is the Self who will need to create the meaning that has significance in life. With this there is "an unshakable joy in this possibility."[97] This is the positive aspect of Angst; we experience the awe and exhilaration that accompanies our recognition that *we* are essentially the creative architects of our own lives. By anticipatorily and resolutely taking hold of our possibilities, it is we who can give it meaning! A person basks in the joyfulness of existence by resolutely taking hold of his or her possibilities in a substantive manner. In this way, individuals achieve authentic existence.

In his book, *Existential Foundations of Medicine and Psychology*, Medard Boss offers a helpful elaboration from a Heideggerian perspective:

> [Joyful serenity] can give human existence the kind of receptivity that allows it to see in the brightest light the meaningfulness and connections of every phenomenon that reveals itself. Such a serenity is a clearness and openness in which a human being is emotionally connected to everything he meets, wanting not to have things in his own power but content to let them be and develop on their own. Because this joyous serenity opens a human being to the broadest possible responsiveness, it constitues happiness as well. For every human existence is by itself attuned to happiness whenever all its innate potential ways of being stand open to it.[98]

The person who experiences joyful serenity can lucidly see the indissoluble interconnectedness of everything within the open field of meaning. Like the Taoists, not wanting to force things to be a certain way, this person is comfortable with letting things be and develop on their own in their everyday

---

[95] Ibid., 179ff.; Heidegger, *History of the Concept of Time*, 283ff.
[96] It is important to note here that Heidegger is not saying that joy eliminates this burden, but rather simply "makes it more bearable." *Being and Time*, 173.
[97] Ibid., 358.
[98] Boss, *Existential Foundations of Medicine and Psychology*, 112.

existence without unnecessary interference.[99]

HOW CAN ONE DASEIN AUTHENTICALLY RELATE TO ANOTHER?

Given that there is a way for the Self to achieve authentic existence, we might inquire how it is possible for us to be authentically with one another. For Heidegger, to answer this question, we must first return to the structure—Being-with—that makes it possible for us to exist within this field of meaning as one involving our capacity to relate to one another.[100] We are co-Daseins within a shared field of meaning. Heidegger writes:

> ...when persons devote themselves to the same affair in common [in this mode]...They thus become *authentically* bound together, and this makes possible the right kind of objectivity which frees the Other in his freedom for himself.[101]

As such, there is a spectrum of possible ways in which we might be said to fundamentally relate to one another. At one extreme of the spectrum, one Dasein is indifferent to other Daseins—others do not matter. At the other extreme, one Dasein actively participates in the shared field of meaning with other Daseins. This happens in one of two opposing ways. On the one hand, one Dasein (X) can leap into another Dasein's (Y) existence and seek to make its decisions for it by imposing (intentionally or unreflectively) X's interpretive framework upon Y. This is what Heidegger describes as "intervening care," and is a form of inauthentic care. On the other hand, Dasein (X) can *leap ahead* of another Dasein's (Y) existence, mutually explore possibilities in order to elucidate them, but most importantly not make choices for the other (Y). This is what Heidegger describes as an authentic way in which two Dasein's can authentically relate—this is called "anticipatory care." It is through anticipatory care that one Dasein (X) can assist another Dasein (Y) in dealing with problems, and yet refrain from imposing anything. This is specifically where Heidegger's phenomenological injunction comes in: "let beings be." It is crucial for Dasein (X) simply to "let the other Dasein (Y) be" in terms of his/her own understanding.

---

[99] This is intrinsic to the Taoist conception of wei-wu-wei—action through inaction. See, Lao Tsu, *Tao Te Ching*, trans. Gia-Fu Feng and Jane English (New York: Vintage Books, 1989).
[100] Heidegger, *Zollikon Seminars*, 157; Heidegger, *Being and Time*, 153-68.
[101] Heidegger, *Being and Time*, 343.

"NOTHING MATTERS"

There is a phrase that we occasionally use in everyday life that nicely illustrates and unifies many of the above themes in Heidegger's early philosophy. It is the phrase: "nothing matters." It both covers up *and* discloses one of the most profoundly significant aspects of human existence.

One of the most fundamental ways in which the "they-self" conceals the experience of Angst is to reduce what it takes to be concerns about "the nothing" to being *nothing more* than a mere platitude: "nothing matters." This expression on the level of public interpretation enables us to remain, curiously enough, in our absorption in the world of beings precisely so that we do not have to face the ultimate disappointment: the lack of foundation to our being. I failed my philosophy exam so "nothing matters." My lover left me so "nothing matters." I lost the sports tournament so "nothing matters." What is especially interesting is that the expression allows us to remain preoccupied with the world of our everyday existence, and thereby shields us from an awareness of a far deeper meaning of this expression.

Yet the irony is that the phrase "nothing matters" simultaneously discloses precisely what it is designed to conceal. (This is an example of being in the truth and the untruth at the same time.) How does it do this? It is in Angst that we gain the authentic recognition that nothing really does *matter*. When Angst discloses "the nothing," we really do come to see that there is no deep meaning or basis to our existence. And *this* really does profoundly matter to us. Now, if existence is to have any meaning or significance whatsoever, *one will have to make it,* one will have to be the genuine architect of his or her own existence—while honestly acknowledging the "givens" of the world—and at the same time realize that there is no foundation.[102] One will have to cope with this "burden of existence" and yet press forward into authentically living life.

Once having truly understood and accepted this given aspect of the human condition, the individual, Heidegger suggests, is in position to see *why "nothing matters" on even a deeper ontological level.* Dasein emerges as existence from the nothing. It is the nothing that makes freedom possible: "freedom is *the abyss of ground* in Dasein."[103] It is the nothing that *makes it possible* for us to relate to being at all, indeed, even to selfhood.[104] It is the nothing that makes all meaning or significance possible at the outset; it is the very "ground of our wonder." It is what makes it possible for us even to ask "why" as we go about coping with the burden of our existence in the first place. Furthermore, we wonder about "the wonder of all wonders"—why there are any beings at all (including human beings).[105] "Why is there

---

[102] It is here that the possibility of nihilism arises.
[103] Heidegger, *Pathmarks,* 134.
[104] Heidegger, *Basic Writings,* 106.
[105] Heidegger, *Pathmarks,* 234.

something rather than nothing?" Hence, "nothing matters" in a far more profound sense than we might ever have imagined!

Three

Stemming the Tide:
Martin Heidegger's Critique of Freudian Psychoanalysis

During the 1930's and 1940's Freudian psychoanalysis was sweeping across Europe as *the* major intellectual influence of the era; it was simply the rage. People were very much taken by the appeal of a theory that could explain so much about human beings on levels that had hitherto remained mysterious and illusive. To put it mildly, Heidegger did not share in this excitement. In fact, this broad phenomenon greatly distressed him on a number of different yet interrelated levels.

First and foremost, on a global scale Heidegger was convinced that psychoanalysis, as a form of science, was being taken as a substitute for philosophy and/or religion.[1] What bothered Heidegger so much about this? He was skeptical about any endeavor to separate the concrete descriptions of human existence from philosophical reflection. To do so, he asseverated, would be a "great self-deception."[2] For this would be to remove such concrete descriptions "from the ontological meaning which sustains them,"[3] something he believed would be disastrous.

Second, scientism, in whatever form, including psychoanalysis, uncritically applied itself to domains inappropriate to its ontological commitments—the realm of human existence. Hence, psychoanalysis, as a manifestation of scientism, which was rapidly becoming *the* dominating theoretical influence throughout the continent, elicited in Heidegger the conviction that this was a time for a call to arms. In Heidegger's assessment of the situation it was critical to stem the tide of "the dictatorship of scientific thinking"[4] of which Freud's metapsychology was a quintessential example. To put it bluntly, Freud's metapsychology was an egregious misapplication of the scientific method to human existence. Hence, Heidegger developed an *extensive* philosophical critique of it as a countervailing force.[5]

From a Heideggerian perspective, seeing science as the only source of knowledge, Freud had uncritically ascribed to its methodological and

---

[1] Petzet, *Encounters and Dialogues with Martin Heidegger*, 49.
[2] Heidegger, *Zollikon Seminars*, 274.
[3] Ibid.
[4] Ibid., 342.
[5] We are able to provide only a brief, relatively elliptical account of Heidegger's critique of Freudian psychoanalysis here. For a more exhaustive analysis see Askay and Farquhar, *Apprehending the Inaccessible*, 192-202, 212-23.

ontological presuppositions. Heidegger was explicit: "Freud's metapsychology is the application of Neo-Kantian philosophy to the human being."[6] The Neo-Kantian position to which Heidegger referred claimed that everything ultimately is grounded in physiology.[7] This position, in turn, had its genesis in the thing-ontology of Cartesianism (with its quest for the development of a unified, comprehensive, *scientific* philosophy)[8] and Kantian epistemology.[9] Given the philosophical context in which Freudian metapsychology emerged, the scientism it uncritically advocated desperately needed to be subjected to a relentless philosophical critique.

What were the most fundamental presuppositions of Freudian metapsychology and why were they problematic?

1. Freud assumed that only "objective" things exist. Here Freud fell prey to a presupposition that extended throughout almost the entire Western philosophical tradition, all the way back to Plato and Aristotle. The focus was on *beings* to be investigated. It was as a result of Descartes powerful influence on modern thinking that this approach became especially dominant. Freud's metapsychology simply reduced human beings to nothing more than just objects of investigation. Heidegger's refrain was that human beings are not objects[10] to be analyzed via scientific methods; to hold the contrary is to miss the very *being* of humans.

2. Freud advocated Cartesian dualism: only two kinds of things exist—the psychical (mind) and the material (body). But if one makes the division between the human mind and body, there is no reasonable way to explain how mind and body interact. Freud was thus forced to contrive a theory to account for their connection: his theory of instincts. The instincts were responsible for the development of mental processes and images. However, according to Heidegger, this was simply to beg the question of the connection between these two realms by merely verbally moving back and forth between psychical and material descriptions of the instincts. No compelling description of the connection between mind and body was ever offered by Freud.

3. Freud asserted that the instincts, Eros and Thanatos, are the ultimate *causes* of all activity. Hence, he advocated a strict *determinism*, and thus concluded that *free will is an illusion*. For example, referring to Freud's *Psychopathology of Everydaylife*, Heidegger noted that Freud held that even

---

[6] Heidegger, *Zollikon Seminars*, 260.
[7] A review of the Neo-Kantian schools, given Heidegger's understanding of psychoanalysis, show that he must have had in mind the Neo-Kantianism of Helmholtz, who argued that physiology is "developed or corrected Kantianism." Helmholtz sought to establish the physiological substratum for all mental events.
[8] Heidegger, *Being and Time*, 128-34.
[9] Heidegger, *Zollikon Seminars*, 207.
[10] Ibid., 153.

parapraxes (e.g., ostensible "slips of the tongue," bungled actions, and so forth) have identifiable causal forces.[11] Heidegger rejected the idea that cause and effect determines human conduct; again, this would be to reduce humans to mere objects. Instead, he argued that there is a much deeper notion of "freedom" which makes possible the very freedom Freud denied. Not only did Heidegger think that Freud was wrong here, but he held that he was wrong *for the wrong reason*. Freud was merely denying a preconceived notion of freedom that is represented in the natural sciences as a non-causal occurrence. But such a narrow conception of freedom preconceives freedom as a *property* of humans, and then obstinately refuses to see any other way of understanding freedom. A more ontologically appropriate way to envision freedom was to regard humans as "open for being claimed by the presence of something."[12] It is the realm in which we live our lives through our openness; causal chains are irrelevant to such a conception of freedom.

4. Freud uncritically adopted the Cartesian subject/object epistemological relation. That is, knowing subjects are related to externally related objects in the world. For Heidegger, such a model misrepresents how we actually *are* in the world—that we more primordially relate to the world as a unified field of meaning.

From these four fundamental presuppositions, Freud then proceeded to contrive various ideas concerning the nature of "psychical" reality—mind— as distinct from the external world. The odd thing, Heidegger noted, is that psychoanalysis inquired "about *processes* and about *changes in the psychical*, but not about *what the psychical is*."[13] As a scientist, Freud was required to offer a clear explanation of just exactly what he meant by the mind as a mechanical thing. This he neglected to accomplish.

The situation was further complicated by the fact that Freud held certain Kantian-like presuppositions: (1) the real natures of the independently existing world and the underlying psychical processes are ultimately unknowable; (2) the ego knows only a phenomenal world; and (3) space and time are forms of thought. From a Heideggerian perspective these all failed because they too were predicated on a contrived subject/object dichotomy and a thing-ontological model. One cannot propose divisions between self and external world or mind and body, claim that both the external world and internal self are unknowable, and yet at the same time insist that this is an adequate explanation of human reality. In other words, given these presuppositions, how can anyone know anything? The mind cannot know a separate body, and neither the mind nor the body can know a separate world, nor can the ego know the inner mysteries of itself, much less an external world

---

[11] Ibid., 5.
[12] Ibid., 217; See also, Heidegger, *Basic Writings*, 126-30.
[13] Heidegger, *Zollikon Seminars*, 20.

completely apart from its existence.   From a Heideggerian standpoint, these
were merely gratuitous hypotheses that exacerbated the situation by further
distorting our understanding of what it means to be a human being.

Freud made other assumptions regarding the function of the psychical
and physical processes as well.   He assumed: (a) that both (psychical and
somatic) domains operated in the same mechanical way;[14] (b) that everything
was ultimately grounded in the somatic forces;[15] (c) that both are involved in a
continuous nexus of causal relations.[16]   Hence, everything is necessarily
subjectable to reductionistic scientistic analysis.[17]   Yet, Heidegger pointed out
that Freud's metapsychology failed on scientific grounds, for it neglected to
satisfy its own methodological criteria.   Freud resorted to unverifiable
presuppositions and non-empirical concepts (e.g., the unconscious, the
instincts, "mythical drives," and so forth).[18]   He also failed to offer—as a
genuine natural scientist must—an adequate account of the relationship
between mind and body, and the transformation of ideas and meanings into
bodily processes.[19]

Heidegger was particularly offended by Freud's position that
everything that exists is measurable.[20]   Or to put it contra-positively, if
something cannot be measured then it does not exist.[21] Heidegger claimed that
science insists on taking *exclusively* that which is measurable and quantifiable
into account.   By doing so, it disregards all other possible characteristic
features of human existence.[22]   This is to preclude the recognition of other
dimensions of human existence that are not susceptible to measurement: for
example, the presencing of being, freedom, the "clearing," and so forth.[23]   If
the physiological level were the basis of human existence, then there would be
"sorrow molecules" or "farewell molecules" in tears.[24]   Yet, Heidegger
insisted: "you can never actually measure tears. If you try to measure them,
you measure a fluid and drops at the most, but not tears."[25]

Furthermore, Freud postulated the complete explainability of
psychical life[26] in causal terms.[27]   His problem was that since no
"uninterrupted explainability" appeared in consciousness, Freud found it

---

[14] Ibid., 24.
[15] Ibid., 233.
[16] Ibid., 7-8.
[17] Ibid., 148; see also, 104.
[18] Ibid., 173; 218-9.
[19] Ibid., 294.
[20] Ibid., 7-8.
[21] Ibid., 6-7; 213.
[22] Ibid., 25-6.
[23] Ibid., 207-8; 80.
[24] Ibid., 7; 155.
[25] Ibid., 81.
[26] Ibid., 260.
[27] Ibid., 148.

necessary to: "invent 'the unconscious.'"[28] According to Heidegger, Freud conceived of the mind as a container,[29] or "a little black box" that is composed of conscious and *unconscious* processes, powered by a form of energy that is analogous to and reciprocally transformable with physical energy; and is ultimately derivable from bodily or organic processes. Hence, even within the mind, Freud made a division between the knower and the unknown knower. The internal mind cannot even know itself. This introduced the "fatal distinction" between the conscious and the unconscious.[30] It was to resort to the hypothesis of "unconscious purposes" as explanations[31] for human motivation.[32]

One of Heidegger's primary criticisms of the unconscious was to point out that Freud conflated "cause" and "motive" in his metapsychology. The two are not the same:[33] "Motive is a reason, and this involves the fact that it is known and represented as such in contrast to a cause which merely acts on its own."[34] Our response to the presence of something is our motive.[35] Given this distinction, it is crucial to see that "Something unconscious cannot be a 'reason for' (i.e., a motive) because such a 'reason for' presupposes conscious awareness. Therefore, the unconscious is unintelligible."[36] Freud's idea of "unconscious intentions" was a pure hypothesis that failed to help us understand any phenomena any better than we could without it—that is, it was dispensable.[37] Instead, Heidegger insisted that acts of forgetting, for example, could be more appropriately explained phenomenologically. They merely indicated that something was no longer considered thematically (i.e., one simply no longer paid explicit attention to its meaning, or chose not to think about it).

All of Freud's theory was riddled with misconceptions and complications. Essentially, they represented nothing more than a desperate attempt by human beings to find a deeper meaning (i.e., a theory of human nature) through which to ground their existence.[38] Yet for Heidegger there is no such ground to human existence. All we are is just a groundless abyss—the nothing. By seeking to provide a ground for human existence, such contrived theories as Freud's wind up losing our very humanity.

---

[28] Ibid., 260.
[29] Ibid., 3-4.
[30] Ibid., 319.
[31] Ibid., 214.
[32] Ibid., 233.
[33] Ibid., 21.
[34] Ibid., 200.
[35] Ibid., 217.
[36] Ibid., 186.
[37] Ibid., 168-69.
[38] In this respect, Freud followed in the footsteps of such philosophical giants as Plato, Aristotle, Schopenhauer, Marx, etc.

In the end, Heidegger took his most serious global criticism of Freud to be that he was simply oblivious to the question of *what it means to be* (i.e., to an understanding of being). Hence he failed to ascertain the true ontological characteristics of human beings.[39] Yet, it was these very characteristics that made any theoretical account (including Freud's) possible in the first place. More specifically, Heidegger claimed that Freud simply failed to see "the clearing,"[40] that each of us always already finds ourselves situated in a unified field of meaning—our Being-in-the-world. In light of this, Freud's theory becomes even more problematic, when one realizes that one cannot construct the significance/meaningfulness of Being-in-the-world from such psychical acts as wishing, urges, propensities, and so forth.[41] Rather, our Being-in-the-world is always *already* presupposed.[42]

---

[39] Heidegger, *Zollikon Seminars*, 282.

[40] Ibid., 228.

[41] Heidegger held that to conceive of ourselves as mechanical beings or things would lead to our no longer being able to account for significance—namely, that anything could matter to us in the first place.

[42] Heidegger, *Zollikon Seminars*, 217-19.

Four

A Creative Misunderstanding:
Ludwig Binswanger

No discourse on the exchange of ideas between Freudian psychoanalysis and philosophical phenomenology would be complete without mentioning the works of psychiatrist, Dr. Ludwig Binswanger. As a one-time mentor to Medard Boss, an acquaintance of Martin Heidegger, and a close friend to Sigmund Freud, Binswanger was thoroughly immersed within the historical context of the time. His continued loyalty to Freud as well as his interest in Husserlian and Heideggerian phenomenology make him an especially pivotal figure in the early intersection between these two domains.

Unlike many of the intellectuals who fervently opposed Freudian psychoanalysis, Binswanger never entirely rejected the importance of Freud's work. He considered Freud's metapsychology to be a success within the limits of scientific theory, and praised its contributions for offering a thorough and complete description of *homo natura*. However, Binswanger also contended that Freud's depiction of humans as "primal" was not "the source and fount of human history," but rather "a requirement of natural-scientific research."[1] Here, Heidegger's philosophy was ideal in demonstrating the limitations of science when practically applied to the realm of human inquiry. His phenomenological approach also offered a means for expanding beyond science in order to understand the whole person in an effort to create a more holistic therapeutic approach.

Early on, (c. 1922–7) Binswanger believed that it was Husserlian phenomenology that could provide the proper method for therapy. With the publication of *Being and Time* in 1927, Binswanger, without entirely abandoning Husserl, modified this somewhat when he suggested that it was Heidegger's ontology from which "existential analysis received its decisive stimulation, its philosophical foundation and justification, as well as its methodological directives."[2] Binswanger was particularly struck by Heidegger's critique of science as well as his elaboration of the universal and fundamental structures of human Dasein.

---

[1] Binswanger, *Being-in-the-World*, 154.
[2] Ludwig Binswanger, "The Existential Analysis School of Thought," trans. Ernest Angel, in *Existence: A New Dimension in Psychiatry and Psychology*, ed. by Rollo May, Ernest Angel, and Henri Ellenberger (New York: Simon and Schuster, 1958), 191; see also, Binswanger, *Being-in-the-World*, 206; Heidegger, *Zollikon Seminars*, 304.

Heidegger's analysis, when applied to the field of psychiatry, revealed a great deal about the particular nature of psychiatry in its attempts to become a science. For it is the business of science to separate out what it intends to study, to remove it of any subjective elements, and to demarcate the territory for scientific research. By adopting this approach, psychiatry runs up against a peculiar problem. Since its "object" of study is that which conducts the research, that is, human beings, it must strip away all that is human in order to approach humans scientifically. Yet, its purpose is not just to "fix" the human organism, but also to heal the human being. The questions arise: is psychiatry to work exclusively within a biological framework, conceiving humans as organisms? Or is psychiatry to deal with humans on a level of human relations? After all, every participant involved is human! Hence, psychiatry appears to engage two "incompatible conceptual horizons"[3] whereby a peculiar dualism, a "mind-body" problem arises. Binswanger believed that the theoretical problem of the mind-body dualism inherent in science introduced a "fatal defect"[4] into all of psychology. Heidegger's "Being-in-the-world," however, provided the saving connection among "subjects" and "world" which would allow for communication and understanding in a shared experience.

Heidegger's underlying universal structure of Being-in-the-world as well as his analysis of the threefold Care structure[5] provided a thorough description of the richness of human existence in "normally" functioning humans. Binswanger was confident that if psychiatry were to begin with Being-in-the-world, it could better understand human interactions that deviated from this "norm."[6] It could shift its focus to consider possible constrictions in the patients' world designs, opening up new channels for relating to "mentally ill" patients who were previously considered unreachable.[7] Such an alternative attitude would also allow psychiatry to

---

[3] Binswanger, *Being-in-the-World*, 209.

[4] Binswanger, "The Existential Analysis School of Thought," 193.

[5] Binswanger described his patients' concrete mode of existence in terms of Heidegger's threefold Care–structure. [See, Binswanger, *Being-in-the-World*, 25-31, 61, 88-91, 101, 116, 211, 250-1; Binswanger, "The Existential Analysis School of Thought," 201, 269, 191, 212, 328; Ludwig Binswanger, *Grundformen und Erkenntnis menschlichen Daseins ("Basic Forms and Cognition of Human Dasein")*, (Zurich: Niehans, 1964), 136ff.] Throughout his writings, he analyzed patients in terms of their idiosyncratic modes of being–in–the–world, their modes of existence in terms of their UmWelt (biological world), MitWelt (communal world), and EigenWelt (self–world) (see, Ludwig Binswanger, "The Case of Ellen West," trans. Werner Mendel and Joseph Lyons, in *Existence: A New Dimension in Psychiatry and Psychology,* ed. by Rollo May, Ernest Angel, and Henri Ellenberger (New York: Simon and Schuster, 1958), 328-29. As such, Heidegger's existentialia were always understood in terms of a concrete process of lived experience.

[6] Binswanger, "The Existential Analysis School of Thought," 201.

[7] Ibid., 192, 200-01.

expand its possibilities toward a more unified approach within the therapeutic setting.[8]

It is important to note that Binswanger considered his efforts to be "phenomenological anthropology," and was clearly aware that his practical application of Heidegger's work was an ontic interpretation of Heidegger's ontological structures. His attempts were apparently well received, even encouraged by Heidegger during the early years of their relationship. In fact, as late as 1947, Heidegger continued to support Binswanger in his endeavors. In a letter dated February 24, 1947, Heidegger praised Binswanger's newest book, entitled *Grundformen und Erkenntnis menschlichen Daseins ("Basic Forms and Cognition of Human Dasein")*: "Your main work is so broadly conceived, and so rich in phenomena, that one should think that anyone who can see must recognize where you locate the entirety of psychopathology."[9] Yet, Heidegger later chastised Binswanger's approach, stressing that *Being and Time* was insufficient for a complete anthropology; he continually emphasized the importance of the "ontological difference," and advised against the temptation to conflate an everyday understanding of human existence (ontic descriptions) with the underlying ontological structures upon which they were grounded.[10]

The early enthusiasm Binswanger exhibited toward Heidegger later gave way to ambivalence. Although he continued to appreciate Heidegger's insights and contributions, in the fourth edition of his book, *Grundformen und Erkenntnis menschlichen Daseins ("Basic Forms and Cognition of Human Dasein")*, Binswanger asserted that Heidegger had simply added a further dimension to Husserl's phenomenology; it was Husserl's later developments of "genetic" and "constititutive" phenomenology that offered the best avenue toward understanding the structures of his patients' worlds. Thus, it was Husserl who had had the greatest impact on his own work.[11] Binswanger also accused Heidegger of neglecting the most primordial social dimension intrinsic to human relating, that of *love*. As Binswanger expressed, "Love is left standing freezing outside the doors of this projection of being."[12]

By taking an individualized "I-ness" of Dasein as his original point of departure, Heidegger failed to account for the more primordial structure of "we-hood" ("we of love" = "being of loving encounter")[13] that constitutes the

---

[8] Ibid., 192.
[9] Binswanger, *Ausgewahlte Werke Band 3*, edited by Max Herzog, (Heidelberg: Asanger Verlag, 1994), 339-40; see also, Roger Frie, *Subjectivity and Intersubjectivity in Modern Philosophy and Psychoanalysis: A Study of Sartre, Binswanger, Lacan, and Habermas* (New York: Rowman and Littlefield, 1997), 82-83.
[10] See Heidegger, *Zollikon Seminars*, esp. 227-28.
[11] Ludwig Binswanger, "Dank an Husserl," in *Edmund Husserl, 1859-1959*, ed. by Van Breda (The Hauge: Nijhoff, 1959), 65.
[12] Binswanger, "The Existential Analysis School of Thought," 195; see also, Heidegger, *Zollikon Seminars*, 304.
[13] Binswanger, *Grundformen*, 29-31.

foundation for human existence in a world of relatedness. Consequently, Heidegger's Care structure of Being-with was restricted to a world of "mine" rather than open to the complete unity of being, a "we-ness."[14] In other words, Binswanger accused Heidegger of imposing limitations on human relatedness because such concerns of Dasein were all too individualized and isolated from their social context of being-in-the-world. Furthermore, any therapeutic approach would likewise be limited to an exploration of authentic versus inauthentic modes of relating to self, world, and others. Yet with severe mental cases, authenticity was of little concern. Such patients often suffered from partial, or, at times, a complete lack of connectedness. Binswanger believed that it was only with the additional structure of *love* that such deficiencies could be thoroughly explored.

Love, according to Binswanger, disclosed an openness toward being which could only most accurately be described as *ours*.[15] Love was understood here as the ontological possibility of "we–hood." In loving coexistence, we are fully engaged in an interdependent presence with the other that is rooted in our very being, yet out of which we "leap beyond" our own singular Dasein.[16] In love, then, we go "beyond" the cares of everyday being–in–the–world, and participate in an "eternal now." For Binswanger, not only was Dasein being–in–the–world as Care, but Dasein was considered being–beyond–the–world in love, that is, being–in–the–world–beyond–the–world (In–der–Welt–uber–die–Welthinaus–sein).[17] Hence, not only was *love* a crucial starting point when looking at the universal and necessary structures underlying human existence; love also provided an additional criteria for helping us to understand better "psychopathological" modes of relating (along with "normal" relating), thereby giving us some indications of the full extent of a patient's restrictedness in his or her relatedness in-the-world.

Binswanger's "positive criticism" and "extension" of Heidegger's structure of being-in-the-world became major points of contention between Binswanger on the one hand, and Heidegger and Boss on the other. Some time during the years 1947-1959 (i.e., the commencement of the Zollikon seminars), Binswanger's and Heidegger's relationship experienced a dramatic shift.[18] In 1957, Boss published a harsh critique of Binswanger's position (as well as Freud's and Jung's) that resulted in the final alienation of Binswanger

---

[14] Others have also made similar arguments regarding the individualistic tendency within *Being and Time:* For example, Max Scheler, *Reality and Resistance* (Evanston: Northwestern University Press, 1927), 63f, 70f.; Georg Lukács, *Marxism and Human Liberation* (London: New Left Books, 1971), 265.
[15] Binswanger, *Grundformen*, 34.
[16] Ibid., 83, 85, 490.
[17] Binswanger, "The Existential Analysis School of Thought," 195; Binswanger, *Being-in-the-World*, 343-45.
[18] It is interesting to note that Heidegger's correspondence with Medard Boss apparently commenced on August 3, 1947, only 6 months after Heidegger's letter of support for Binswanger's book, *Grundformen*. See Heidegger, *Zollikon Seminars*, 237.

from his two eminent colleagues. During the entire 25-year span in which Heidegger conducted the Zollikon seminars, he had nothing but criticisms and admonitions for Binswanger and his form of Daseinsanalysis. Most certainly, both Heidegger and Boss took every opportunity to attack Binswanger for his "subjectivistic revision of 'Daseinsanalytic' approach."[19] And any questions from Zollikon participants involving Binswanger were met with disparaging answers. Heidegger was clear: "Binswanger shows this complete misunderstanding of my thinking in the most striking way in his huge book *Grundformen und Erkenntnis menschlichen Daseins*...all the ontic ways of comportment of those who love...are grounded equiprimordially in *being-in-the-world* as *care*. If one does not confuse ontological insights with ontic matters as Binswanger did, then there is likewise no need to speak about a 'being-beyond-the-world.'"[20]

Binswanger admitted to his confusion, deeming his misinterpretation of Heidegger's analytic of Dasein a "creative misunderstanding."[21] Nonetheless, Binswanger's "psychiatric Daseinanalysis,"[22] or "existential analysis," made its own unique contribution to the field of psychiatry.

---

[19] Boss, *Psychoanalysis and Daseinsanalysis*, 51.

[20] Heidegger, *Zollikon Seminars*, 227-28.

[21] Binswanger, *Grundformen*, 121; Binswanger, "The Existential Analysis School of Thought," 195; Heidegger, *Zollikon Seminars*, 115.

[22] Heidegger makes the distinction between Binswanger's *"psychiatric* Daseinsanalysis" and Heidegger's/Boss' "Daseinsanalysis" so as not to confuse the two schools of thought. (*Zollikon Seminars*, 113n, 115). Interestingly, Binswanger was the first to use the term, "Daseinsanalysis" in regards to his new psychoanalysis—a term Boss later adopted as well—but, as we have seen, Heidegger and Boss felt the need to distance themselves from Binswanger after his "extension" of Heidegger's Care structure.

Five

In Search of a Humanistic Grounding for Psychoanalysis:
Medard Boss

Under the vigilant authority of Martin Heidegger, Dr. Medard Boss conspired to bring about the transformation in psychoanalytic thinking that Heidegger so passionately desired. Although the date of their initial encounter is unclear,[1] their friendship and collegial relationship endured until the end of their lives. Boss, who was classically trained by both Ludwig Binswanger and Sigmund Freud in psychoanalysis, praised Heidegger for having had the greatest influence on his work. In the preface of his book, *Existential Foundations of Medicine and Psychology,* Boss gave much credit to his long time friend and colleague: " . . . this work actually evolved under Heidegger's watchful eye. There is not one section of 'philosophical' import which was denied his generous criticism."[2] Indeed, a copy of a couple pages of Heidegger's extensive corrections to Boss' book was included in *Heidegger & Psychology*.[3] In turn, Boss helped Heidegger to extend his reach beyond the confines of philosophy, into the inner circles of medicine. He was responsible for the initiation, execution, and publication of the *Zollikon Seminars*— lectures presented by Heidegger in Boss's home—in an attempt to help other

---

[1] It is not altogether clear exactly when and how Boss first came into contact with Heidegger and/or his work. Boss was a "one-time student" of Binswanger, (Frie, *Subjectivity and Intersubjectivity*, 83) and most likely learned of Heidegger through this mutual connection. [Spiegelberg wrote that it was Binswanger who first drew Boss' attention to Heidegger—Herbert Spiegelberg, *Phenomenology in Psychology and Psychiatry: A Historical Introduction* (Evanston: Northwestern University Press, 1972), 335-36.] Boss did give credit to Binswanger in *Existential Foundations of Medicine and Psychology*: "Modern psychopathology owes a special debt to Binswanger for drawing its attention to his [Heidegger's] thought." (p. 71.) Yet in the *Zollikon Seminars*, Boss claimed that he just happened to see an advertisement for *Sein und Zeit (Being and Time)* in a newspaper clipping, and that he first wrote to Heidegger in 1947, "shortly after the end of the war." (p. xxxiv). In addition, in *Heidegger & Psychology*, Boss wrote, "Thanks to the wonder that Martin Heidegger—who received yearly hundreds of letters from different parts of the world and answered scarcely a one of them—found my very first written communication worthy of an extremely warm response. That was *1946*." (p. 7—authors' italics.)
[2] Boss, *Existential Foundations*, xxiv.
[3] Hoeller, Heidegger and Psychology.

medical professionals to "see differently" and "think anew."[4] Both Heidegger and Boss were critical of the newly evolving religion, called "science," and sought to salvage the remnants of humanity in their critique and development of a new psychoanalysis which later became known as "Daseinsanalysis."

One of the prime perpetrators guilty of the misapplication of scientific methodology to the realms of human inquiry was Sigmund Freud. Both Heidegger and Boss vehemently opposed Freud's metapsychology. Here Boss launched similar criticisms against Freud as Heidegger had, claiming that Freud's Cartesian dualism formed an unbridgeable gap which served only to impede any profound understanding of human existence. Freud's metapsychology should dispense with any notions that created an unrealistic picture of humans as "having" an internal and external component,[5] and psychoanalysts should resist the temptation to create psychological "black boxes" within the human psyche. Instead medicine should appeal to immediate experience. What immediate experience actually revealed, according to Boss, was a realization that human beings are "always and from the beginning" fulfilling their existence "in and as one or the other mode of behavior in regard to something or somebody."[6]

Although Boss' rejection of Freud's metapsychology was absolute, early in his career Boss remained sympathetic to much of Freud's therapeutic approach. Rather than dispensing with all of Freudian psychoanalysis, Boss proposed that Freud's work was "split" between his theoretical methodology and therapeutic practice. He argued that Freud's theory was inconsistent with his therapeutic advice, both on the level of reason and through his own experience of Freudian psychoanalysis. As a former analysand of Freud's, and a trained Freudian psychoanalyst himself, Boss had come to know Freud as a person as well as his theoretical work. Although he rejected Freud's scientific methodology, he had faith in the efficacy of Freud's techniques and understanding of the therapeutic process. He understood Freud-the-therapist as a kind, caring person[7] who always had the best interest of his patients in

---

[4] Heidegger, *Zollikon Seminars*, xix.

[5] For example, Boss rejects much of Freud's theory, including: "ideas" existing in or contained within a "psychical apparatus;" "dynamic energy" which is transformed in unexplainable ways; the existence of an "unconscious;" theoretical constructs such as "repression" and "resistance;" a theory of dreams which includes "wishfulfilments" of "latent dream thoughts," and reduced "dream images" to symbolic representations, and so forth. See, Boss, *Psychoanalysis and Daseinsanalysis*, 75-129; Boss, *Existential Foundations*: psychic apparatus, 35-6; dynamic, 136; unconscious 135-43; repression 243-47; Boss, M. *Analysis of Dreams*, trans. Arnold Pomerans (London: Rider, 1957), 32-49.

[6] Boss, *Psychoanalysis and Daseinsanalysis,* 33.

[7] At the authors' home in 1989, Boss reminisced about his years as a student and analysand to Sigmund Freud. It was apparent that Boss was quite fond of his therapist. He insisted that Freud-the-therapist was a warm and loving man, and an amazing

mind, and he understood that Freud's primary focus was on creating a non-intrusive environment that was open to the natural unfolding of the therapeutic process. Boss believed that if one were able to grasp fully the ramifications of Freud's practical advice on therapy, one would uncover a closeted Heideggerian.

Boss' revelations of the intrinsic harmony between Heidegger's analysis of Dasein, and Freud's therapeutic advice was presented in his book, *Psychoanalysis and Daseinsanalysis*. Here Boss exposed the underlying presuppositions in Freudian therapy that Freud himself had neglected to see,[8] and had unwittingly concealed because of his uncritical loyalties to science. Boss argued, for instance, that Freud's fundamental rule of psychoanalysis—the requirement that patients must always approach therapy with absolute honesty and truthfulness—revealed that Freud's therapy aimed at "enabling the patient to unveil himself and to unfold into his utmost openness."[9] Such an aim was only consistent if one presupposed Dasein as *openness*. Similarly, by focusing on the meaning content of dreams as well as all human phenomena, "Freud-the-therapist" must have held a non-causal conception of human beings, since obviously the meaning dimension of human existence is incompatible and exclusive of scientific causality. Thus, Freud necessarily presupposed something akin to "a luminated realm into the lucidity of which the meaningfulness of our world's phenomena can disclose itself, shine forth,"[10] and it was "human existence itself which serves as this necessary, elucidating world-openness."[11]

Not only did Freud-the-therapist conceive of humans as *openness*; he obviously believed that humans had an ability to exercise their human freedom (i.e., the freedom to make choices regarding how one will live one's life),[12] and ultimately to decide whether to live an authentic or inauthentic existence (which was consistent with Heidegger's conceptualization of human potentiality-for-being). Again, this was clearly demonstrated in Freud's explicit instructions regarding who could and could not benefit from psychoanalysis. Individuals with serious flaws in character or who were lacking in intelligence could not be helped; only those people capable of making choices would most likely be in a position to reap the benefits of therapy. In addition, *resistance* in therapy—a frequently considered topic in psychoanalysis—surely indicated that Freud acknowledged the possibility that

---

therapist who never actually related to his analysands as the cold, detached scientist his writings appear to endorse.

[8] This is precisely in line with Heidegger's "reinterpretation" of previous historical figures he perceived to be approaching (albeit unknowingly) crucial ontological insights (e.g., Kant).

[9] Boss, *Psychoanalysis and Daseinsanalysis*, 62.

[10] Ibid., 65.

[11] Ibid.

[12] It should be noted that Boss misinterpreted both Heidegger's and Freud's conception of "freedom."

individuals had the capacity to flee from selfhood. After all, the primary purpose of therapy was to offer patients choices on whether to flee or to embrace their own most possibility for authentic existence.

In order thoroughly to explore the horizons of patients' possibilities, Freud approached his analysands as an historian, examining their life histories in order to make sense of their present situations, and he emphasized the importance of childhood experiences in uncovering past trauma. This was an indication to Boss that Freud actually had an awareness of the importance of historicity and temporality similar to Heidegger's. Furthermore, Freud's emphasis on the permissiveness of the therapeutic environment, his insistence that the therapist remain non judgmental, and his warnings against imposing ones' theoretical understandings on patients, all suggested that Freud had an understanding of Heidegger's distinction between "intervening" versus "anticipatory" care. Both great thinkers had obviously recognized these two modes of human relatedness, and advocated the latter.

With the proper grounding of Freudian therapy in Heideggerian ontology, Boss believed that the most valuable aspects of psychoanalysis could be saved, more fully appreciated, and even expanded into a unified and holistic therapeutic approach. Borrowing from Ludwig Binswanger, Boss named his new psychoanalysis, "Daseinsanlysis," and he set about to reexamine how medicine was to proceed.

Boss began with an inquiry into pathology. In order to understand pathology in Dasein, one must first be clear as to what is meant by health. Only then can one build a truly effective therapeutic framework. Freud's dynamic view of human nature reduced both health and pathology to an interplay of conflicting forces and energies. Yet, this was not at all how Boss believed humans truly experienced life, nor was it an adequate characterization of suffering. Rather, his investigations had revealed a new description of humans as being openness, world-illuminating, temporal beings, who are free to choose their mode of existence, and who are either authentic (anticipatory care) or inauthentic (intervening care) in their comportment towards self, world, and others. Illness was redefined as restrictedness in relating. Boss proposed three central questions when evaluating a patient's being-in-the-world: (1) How is a person's freedom to carry out her or his potentialities impaired at any given time?; (2) What are these potentialities?; and (3) With respect to which entities of the person's world does this impairment occur?[13]

With a new focus for therapy and an understanding of illness as world constrictedness, Boss reexamined aspects of Freud's therapeutic approach. He found several contaminated remnants buried beneath Freud's scientific grounding. For instance, Freud's scientific perspective had tainted his view of therapy, conceiving it as a form of transference whereby patients regressed to earlier childhood repetitions, acting out on therapists as the intended love-objects. As such, he advocated adopting the "surgeon's" objective and cold

---

[13] Boss, *Existential Foundations*, 200.

mannerisms toward patients in order to allow transference to occur—providing a blank slate upon which the patients could project their pasts—and to avoid counter-transference. Psychoanalysts were discouraged from becoming emotionally involved with their patients, since such personal entanglements could seriously complicate and hinder the therapeutic process. This was in complete opposition to Boss who insisted that the therapeutic relationship must be considered "genuine," and not simply an act of transference. It was only through the development of authentic, respectful, and loving relationships that patients could come to trust their analysts and feel safe to "act out" in necessary ways. If therapists maintained an "objective" stance, as Freud had suggested, it could serve to frustrate the patients' "acting out" and discourage them from revealing themselves as childish—resulting in an imposed restriction that could severely impede therapeutic progress.[14]

Boss stressed that patients' acting-out was not a repetition at an intended love-object, but an original unfolding that was not possible prior to the trusting analyst-analysand relationship. Only within the safety of therapy would patients be enabled to overcome their restricted world-relations and experience new possibilities of relating.[15] Hence, whereas Freud saw transference as a necessary "regression" to early childhood, Boss emphasized that there could be no return; such patients never developed beyond their childish ways of relating. At most, they only learned to disguise their infant-like ways, masquerades that often revealed highly restricted world-relations. What Daseinsanalysis could do, was provide the opportunity for patients to experience a "genuine parent-child relationship," *for the first time,* so that they could heal past wounds, and eventually mature to the level of responsible adults.[16]

Freud's scientific heritage also obscured his therapeutic vision when it came to various phenomena such as hallucinations and dreams. Freud placed too much emphasis on what is "real" as opposed to "phantasy." Rather than question the reality of a patients' experiences, or attempting to restrict patients' "hallucinations" and dreams in the realm of "manifestations of sickness," Boss asserted, "We *have* no dreams; we *are* our dreaming state..."[17] Why not approach hallucinations and dreams as "equally autonomous and 'real,' although different, way(s) of behaving and of relating to what is shining

---

[14] Boss, *Psychoanalysis and Daseinsanalysis*, 238-40.

[15] Ibid., 233-47.

[16] It should also be mentioned that although Boss acknowledged the value of Freud's focus on childhood trauma, he asserted that at times Freud's overemphasis on the past could potentially limit patients by imposing an expectation that they *must* remember the childhood traumas that were responsible for their illnesses (Boss, *Psychoanalysis and Daseinsanalysis,* 243). Instead of focusing exclusively on past trauma, Boss advocated an emphasis on the "primacy" of the future; since Dasein *is* its possibilities, the therapeutic focus should not neglect futural ecstasis.

[17] Ibid., 261.

forth in the light of Dasein."[18]   What was truly important was what "hallucinations" and dreams revealed about patients' world-relations, and any restrictions on possibilities. By simply accepting various human "happenings" such as dreams as meaningful, analysts were afforded access to important insights regarding their patients' waking states.[19]

Boss was aware (and had argued this point) that Freud also emphasized the value of the meaning-content inherent in dreams. Both believed in the power of dreams for unveiling some of the mysteries of human existence, and both considered dreams to be powerful therapeutic tools for bringing about awareness.[20] However, Boss strongly disapproved of Freud's dream theory. He was particularly disturbed by Freud's division of the *manifest* and *latent* dream content; as though the "real meaning" of a dream could be hidden beneath the distorted façade of a manifest dream. Such a bifurcation distorted the profound significance of dreams, and reduced Freud's dream analysis to "reconstructions of latent dream thoughts,"[21] something Boss believed to be nothing more than arbitrary interpolations by analysts. Boss was adamant: "In these reconstructions of latent dream thoughts Freud has without doubt opened wide the doors to arbitrariness and violence to the facts."[22] He characterized Freud's dream interpretation as "dogmatic" and reductionistic—the dream, in essence, being reducible to wish-fulfillments of unconscious infantile instinctual desires.[23] As with any and all meaningful human experiences, Boss proposed instead that therapists approach dreams in their immediacy, allowing the phenomena to "appear and to develop according to their own nature."[24]

Boss' fundamental shift in his understanding and approach to therapy opened the doors for a more holistic and unified psychotherapy. In 1970, Boss (along with Gion Condrau)—with Heidegger's blessing and encouragement—established the Swiss Society for Daseinsanalysis in Zurich, and in 1971, the Zurich Institute for Daseinsanalytic Psychotherapy and Psychosomatics, later known as the Medard Boss Foundation. Subsequently, the Swiss Professional Federation for Daseinsanalysis was founded in Zurich in 1984, continuing the tradition that Boss had inspired, and fulfilling a wish Heidegger had disclosed to his friend so many years in the past—that Heidegger's "thinking would escape the confines of the philosopher's study and become of benefit to wider circles, in particular to a large number of suffering human beings."[25]

---

[18] Ibid.
[19] Ibid., 262; see also, Boss, *Existential Foundations*, 169; Boss, *Analysis of Dreams,* 207-11.
[20] Boss, *Analysis of dreams*, 26-27.
[21] Ibid., 32.
[22] Ibid.
[23] Ibid., 29.
[24] Ibid., 119.
[25] Hoeller, *Heidegger and Psychology*, 7; see also, Heidegger, *Zollikon Seminars*, xvii.

Conclusion:
Toward an Integration of Psychoanalysis and Phenomenological Ontology

It is interesting to note that psychology did not emerge as a separate discipline from philosophy until the 19th Century. Arguably, Sigmund Freud was a primary contributor to this division. His adherence to scientific methodology quickly became one of the major points of contention between psychoanalysis and phenomenological philosophy. For although Freud was utterly convinced that his metapsychology could serve as the basis for philosophical thought (as well as all human inquiry), Martin Heidegger was appalled by the use of scientism as a vehicle for understanding the *meaning* of human existence. Heidegger insisted that it was philosophy that grounded our understanding of any being whatsoever. In this regard, it appears that the old adage "never the twain shall meet" aptly applies. However, further investigation reveals the possibility of a complementary relationship between Freud and Heidegger's worldviews, one that enables a more holistic understanding of human beings in general.

It was the Swiss psychoanalysts, Ludwig Binswanger and Medard Boss who were among the first to consider the possibility that psychoanalysis and phenomenology were not entirely mutually exclusive, as the two traditions had assumed. Yet, the approaches of both are open to devastating criticism from both a Heideggerian and Freudian perspective. Binswanger's adaptation of Heidegger's analysis of *Being and Time* resulted in a "creative misunderstanding" in which he developed a form of philosophical anthropology. From a Heideggerian point of view, Binswanger placed far too much emphasis on an ontical analysis of human existence while remaining ostensibly oblivious to the crucial ontological dimension of the human condition.[1] On the other hand, Freud considered Binswager's work to be merely a demonstration of esoteric philosophical abstraction. Boss—who was more faithful to Heidegger's goals than Binswanger—attempted to merge psychoanalysis and Heideggerian phenomenology by focusing on what he claimed to be the pivotal conception of freedom. Unfortunately, Boss' endeavors both ignored the primacy of Heidegger's ontological conception of freedom as the basis for his concern with existential freedom, and completely misconstrued Freud's conception of freedom as involving any kind of existential choice at all. The result is that despite their valiant attempts, Binswanger and Boss failed to establish harmonious relations between Heidegger's philosophy and Freud's psychoanalysis.

---

[1] Heidegger, *Zollikon Seminars*, 151.

There is yet another way to establish a rapprochement between psychoanalysis and phenomenological ontology. Arguably it was Friedrich Nietzsche (functioning as a psychologist) who first provided a truly substantive answer. For it was he who perspicaciously and insistently underscored the importance of identifying the *motives* (as they are grounded in our instincts) for why one holds the philosophical position one does.[2] For this reason, he held that "psychology is now the path to the fundamental problems."[3] Freud was in complete agreement. This is why he developed his idea of conducting "psychographies" on many great thinkers. "In no other science does the personality of the scientific worker play anything like so large a part as in philosophy. A psychography teaches us to recognize *the affective units*—the complexes dependent on the instincts...psychoanalysis can indicate subjective and individual motives behind philosophical theories..."[4]

Freud did not himself factually apply this idea to Heidegger specifically. However, it is interesting to note that Freud's one time protégé, Carl Jung did precisely this in the *spirit* of Freud's point:

> Heidegger's *modus philosophandi* is neurotic through and through and is ultimately rooted in his psychic crankiness...Philosophy still has to learn that it is *made by human beings* and depends to an alarming degree on their psychic constitution. ...There is no thinking *qua* thinking, *at times it is a pisspot of unconscious devils*, just like any other function that lays claim to hegemony. Often what is thought is less important than *who* thinks it. But this is assiduously overlooked. Neurosis addles the brain of every philosopher because he is at odds with himself. His philosophy is then nothing but a systematized struggle with his own uncertainty.[5]

---

[2] Friedrich Nietzsche, *The Portable Nietzsche*, trans. and ed. by Walter Kaufmann (New York: Viking Press, 1970), 670. See also, Friedrich Nietzsche, *Beyond Good and Evil: Prelude to a Philosophy of the Future,* trans. Walter Kaufmann (New York: Vintage Books, 1989), 11; Friedrich Nietzsche, *The Will to Power*, trans Walter Kaufmann and R.J. Hollingdale (New York: Vintage Books, 1968), 25. Ultimately, this position is traceable back to Schopenhauer's philosophy which had impacted Nietzsche a great deal (see Askay and Farquhar, *Apprehending the Inaccessible*, 139-52).

[3] Nietzsche, *Beyond Good and Evil*, 32.

[4] Freud, *SE* XIII, 179.

[5] Sigmund Freud, and Carl Jung, *Freud/Jung Correspondence*, Vol. 1 (Princeton: Princeton University Press, 1974), 331-2. On the very last point, Heidegger would have agreed with Jung: "Philosophy constantly remains in the perilous neighborhood of supreme uncertainty." (Heidegger, *Fundamental Concepts of Metaphysics*, 19.) On the very last point, Heidegger would have agreed with Jung: "Philosophy constantly remains in the perilous neighborhood of supreme uncertainty." (Heidegger, *Fundamental Concepts of Metaphysics*, 19.)

It is because the ideas we generate are contingent upon our psychological constitutions, that "Freud" is able to stand back and provide a cogent analysis of Heidegger's unconscious motivations in the context of the play, *Of Philosophers and Madmen*. Understanding a thinker's psychic constitution contributes a great deal to understanding the functioning of certain philosophical ideas within a philosopher's worldview.[6]

In addition, Heidegger's philosophy has its own potential contributions for psychoanalysis. For instance, it provides a cogent analysis of the ontological conditions which are presupposed and make it possible for us to have any meaning whatsoever (e.g., it can account for how it was possible for Freud to generate his theory in the first place). Heidegger provides an ontological grounding for the spatiality, temporality, sexuality, and so forth of the "body-ego" to which Freud alludes. It can also provide an alternative, yet complementary account to Freud's regarding how concealment is the inaccessible manifesting itself to us. In addition, Heidegger notes that one of the original meanings for the ancient Greek sense of the word "analysis" was to engage in a "freeing activity" in the sense of liberating a person from captivity.[7] His analysis serves to free analysts and analysands from their unreflectively held ontological commitments—to "let beings be," free from any "dogmatic constructions" and conceptual impositions. This offers the opportunity for everyone to be truly open to *whatever presences itself* in the *way it* presences itself. This would enable individuals to have a greater horizon of possibilities in which they could achieve genuine self-knowledge.

ANALYZING HEIDEGGER

In the opening act of the play, *Of Philosophers and Madmen*, Heidegger appears to be unresponsive, intensely anxious, depressed, and distraught.

---

[6] It is important to note in the above that Freud and Jung were careful *not* to suggest that *all* philosophical reflection is *reducible* to unconscious motivations, but merely to draw our attention to the crucial role that they play in the development of those reflections. (Freud, *SE* XIII, 178-79.) Why is this important? It is customary for philosophers to reject Freud's/Jung's positions as necessarily involving what they call "the genetic fallacy:" confusing the causal origins of an idea with its justification or its truth/falsity. However, neither of them denied that there is a significant difference between the validity of philosophical idea/position *x* and the psychological origins that lead a person to hold philosophical idea/position *x*. Their point is even though there is this difference, it does not follow that we should ignore the underlying factors for how it was that *x* was developed originally. Certainly the latter is not necessarily relevant as to whether *x* is logically sound or unsound, but the latter does contribute to our understanding as to why *x* arose in the first place in a particular person. The latter can certainly enhance our understanding and appreciation of that person and of the meaning of *x* for that person's *intellectual and emotional development*. This is precisely how Freud proceeded in the context of our play.
[7] Heidegger, *Zollikon Seminars*, 114.

When he does respond he seems to do so with non-sequiturs and phrases that indicate a great deal of distress (e.g., compulsively reiterating "nothing matters"). Heidegger ostensibly hears voices, feels as if people are out to get him, feels misunderstood and a dissolution of a sense of self, is obsessively preoccupied with alien ideas, couches his language in strange abstractions, and so forth. Based on this evidence it might be natural to conclude that we have a world-famous philosopher who appears to be suffering from some form of mental disorder.

This concrete, albeit fictitious, historical engagement between Heidegger and psychoanalysis affords us the opportunity to reconsider what we believe to be the relationship between philosophical worldviews and what we have come to define as mental disorders (ranging from neurosis to psychosis). Is there potentially an identifiable correlation between the two? Why is it that the one can be so easily mistaken for the other? Most specifically, why is it eminent philosophers typically have depressive personalities?

It was Aristotle who first took note of this last question: "Why is it that all those who have become eminent in philosophy...are clearly of an *atrabilious* temperament and some of them to such an extent as to be affected by diseases."[8] He is also famous for his quote that "genius always contains a touch of madness."[9]   Aristotle's remarks have been born out when one considers that this has been true of a disproportionately high percentage of the most prominent philosophical geniuses throughout the Western tradition. For example, all of the following are known to have had personalities that were severely depressive and/or suicidal: Pascal, Voltaire, Hume, Rousseau, Kant, Hegel, Schopenhauer, Nietzsche, Mill, Kierkegaard, Comte, James, Santayana, Russell, Wittgenstein, Husserl, and Camus.[10] Heidegger too, of course, can be added to the list.

Recall that from a Freudian point of view, "the mental life of the child is important for the psychological understanding of philosophical concepts."[11] One might wonder whether there was a specific type of traumatic event in childhood which most of these eminent thinkers had in common. For example, many of the most prominent philosophers had lost one or both parents during childhood: Montaigne, Hobbes, Descartes, Pascal, Spinoza, Leibniz, Voltaire, Hume, Rousseau, Kant, Hegel, Schopenhauer, Nietzsche, Russell, Sartre.   Almost all of whom are on the list of those who had

[8] Richard Gregory, ed., *The Oxford Companion to The Mind* (Oxford: Oxford University Press, 1987), 371.
[9] George Seldes, ed., *The Great Thoughts* (New York: Ballantine Books, 1985), 20.
[10] Ben-Ami Scharfstein, *The Philosophers: Their Lives and the Nature of Their Thought* (Oxford: Oxford University Press, 1980), 346.
[11] Freud, *SE* XIII, 185.

melancholic personalities.[12] The correlation is far too high to be ignored and probably had at least some impact on the development of their philosophies.

It is widely known that Heidegger's melancholic states were not confined to his mental collapse in 1947. His major biographer, Rüdiger Safranski, reported that in numerous episodes sprinkled throughout his life, Heidegger found himself in deep depression.[13] In the *Zollikon Seminars*, Boss described how Heidegger would sporadically slip into the depths of profound depression during some of their vacations together. Hannah Arendt referred to Heidegger's "recurring periods of depression."[14] The evidence suggests that Heidegger clearly had a depressive personality. However, unlike the other eminent philosophers above, Heidegger did not lose a parent during childhood. He was 35 and 38 when his father and mother died, respectively. Hence, for Freud we would have to look for other kinds of evidence of trauma in his childhood.

One particularly prominent feature of Heidegger's early life that clearly stands out was his tumultuously *ambivalent* relationship with the Catholic Church. Heidegger's parents had instilled the values of Catholicism in him at a very early age. He reported, however, that he was "ashamed" because he was forced to adapt to it based on his financial dependence for his education.[15] Yet, as late as 1910, Heidegger said that he still believed that the Church's "treasure of truth" was a gift.[16] He subsequently developed a critique of Catholic philosophy that he dared not risk uttering publicly.[17] He wrote, "the *system* of Catholicism is problematic and unacceptable to me,"[18] and in his mid-twenties he claimed that Catholicism as the "treasure of truth" was an illusion.[19] Yet, Heidegger reported that severing his relations with his Catholic origins had been very "painful."[20] As Safranski put it: "the conflict with the faith of his origin" was one of the "very troublesome stakes" sticking in his flesh.[21] Heidegger's parents were aghast, to say the least, at his rejection of Catholicism in his mid-twenties.[22] Indeed, when his mother was dying in 1927, Heidegger recounted how it pained him to be regarded by his "pious mother as a son who has lapsed from the *faith*."[23]

From a Freudian standpoint, Heidegger clearly grew up in a highly moralistic historical setting. It is one that was likely to have clashed with his

---

[12] Scharfstein, *The Philosophers*, 346.
[13] Safranski, *Martin Heidegger*, 40, 216, 354, 379.
[14] Ettinger, *Hannah Arendt/Martin Heidegger*, 85-86.
[15] Safranski, *Martin Heidegger*, 10, 41, 43, 46, 47, 59.
[16] Ibid., 22.
[17] Ibid., 65.
[18] Ibid., 107.
[19] Ibid., 109-11.
[20] Ibid., 272.
[21] Ibid., 314.
[22] Ibid., 69-70.
[23] Ibid., 144.

libidinal urges. Indeed Heidegger himself so much as acknowledged this tension in his own existence: "And do you want a spiritual life? Do you want to gain your happiness? *Then die, kill the base things in you,* work with supernatural grace and you will be resurrected."[24] Heidegger also said: "To be primitive means to stand, from an inner urge and drive at the point where things begin to be primitive, to be driven by internal forces."[25] It is interesting to juxtapose these remarks with letters to Hannah Arendt during the years of their affair: "We have been allowed to meet: we must hold that as a gift in our innermost being and avoid deforming it through self deception about the purity of living."[26] He openly referred to the "demonic" within him that struck during their relationship,[27] and in a letter to Arendt he spoke of the importance of "keeping [his] instincts under control."[28] Again: "...my longing for you is becoming less and less controllable."[29] "What no one ever appreciates is how experimenting with oneself and, for that matter, all compromises, techniques, *moralizing*, escapism, and closing off one's growth can only inhibit and distort the providence of being."[30] Hence, it was crucial for Heidegger to keep this affair secret from everyone—his wife, parents, the Messkirch community, and most of all, the Catholic Church, since it was its values that informed almost everyone. This is why Heidegger insisted on "absolute secrecy"[31] and sent cryptic notes to Arendt, which he requested that she destroy.

Interestingly, it was Freud who offered a clear and cogent explanation for characteristics similar to Heidegger's psychological tensions in his book, *Civilization and Its Discontents*:

> ...in many adults...the place of the father or the two parents is taken by the larger human community. Consequently, such people habitually allow themselves to do any bad thing which promises them enjoyment, so long as they are sure that the authority will not know anything about it or cannot blame them for it; they are afraid only of being found out.[32]

> ...the conscience is the immediate expression of fear of the external authority, a recognition of the tension between the ego and that

---

[24] Victor Farias, *Heidegger and Nazism,* trans. Paul Burrell and Gabriel Ricci (Philadelphia: Temple University Press, 1989), 43.
[25] Ibid., 231. It is important to note that this quote comes from an entirely different context within which Heidegger is arguing in support of National Socialism in 1933. It is still revealing since Heidegger's general position was to reject the existence of such urges over the course of his career.
[26] Ettinger, *Hannah Arendt/Martin Heidegger,* 4.
[27] Ibid., 6.
[28] Ibid., 17.
[29] Ibid., 22.
[30] Ibid., 25.
[31] Safranski, *Martin Heidegger,* 137.
[32] Freud, *SE* XXI, 125.

authority. It is the direct derivative of the conflict between the need for the authority's love and the urge towards instinctual satisfaction...[33]

From a Freudian viewpoint, it is relatively clear that the above tension formed a pivotal part of the background of Heidegger's historical trajectory.

Given Heidegger's circumstances, an obvious question to ask is whether he might have consciously experienced guilt in relation to the historical context of his affair. In one respect, Heidegger privately acknowledged his guilt to Arendt: he described "*his* guilt" for having concealed his affair with Arendt from his wife in his second letter to Arendt after their reconciliation in 1950.[34] However, other than this, there does not appear to be any evidence that Heidegger experienced conscious guilt in this matter. Freud would suggest at this point that we look for actions that might indicate *unconscious* guilt. On this question, Heidegger's biographer, Safranski, makes an intriguing observation, and then a highly suggestive speculation: "The fact that Heidegger in, of all places, his letter to Elisabeth Blochman addresses the aspect of evil in the Nothing (i.e., the Nothing includes *temptation by evil*)—could this have something to do with an irresistible feeling that he is a seducer?"[35] Later Safranski added: "there are those who, hungry for intensity and oblivious of morality, allow themselves to experience evil like some strangely alluring wild experience."[36] Heidegger's affair with Arendt would seem to fit the bill precisely.

PHILOSOPHY AND MADNESS

A few contemporary philosophers and psychologists have also noted a certain affinity between philosophy and mental disorders (or madness). In the 19th century, contrary to Fichte's claim that genius (especially of the philosophical kind) and madness were opposite poles of humankind, Schopenhauer (following Plato and Democritus) argued they actually enjoy a close "kinship" that include metaphysical epiphanies and/or loss that transcend ordinary everyday experience.[37] This is especially manifested as a loss of connection to the present and/or particulars of everyday experience. In fact, the two most important and influential philosophers of the twentieth century—Wittgenstein and Heidegger—both explicitly made this precise observation, albeit on different levels. For instance, Wittgenstein wrote that at times, "the philosopher is the man who has to cure himself of many sicknesses of the

---

[33] Ibid., 137.
[34] Ettinger, *Hannah Arendt/Martin Heidegger*, 58.
[35] Safranski, *Martin Heidegger,* 181.
[36] Ibid., 183.
[37] Schopenhauer, *World as Will and Representation*, vol. 1, 191-3.

understanding..."[38] One standard interpretation of Wittgenstein on this score
is that philosophers tend to have an obsessive-compulsive predilection for
metaphysical speculation and abstraction that he arguably saw as a kind of
illness in need of immediate therapy. "The real discovery is the one that
makes me capable of stopping doing philosophy when I want to—The one that
gives philosophy peace, so that it is no longer tormented by questions which
itself brings in question."[39]

Throughout the *Zollikon Seminars*, Heidegger noticed that the
exclusionary and dominating philosophical perspective on the nature of human
existence of the modern age hyper-rationality and scientism (the obsession
with these he saw as a form of madness on a global scale) were mirrored in the
mental disorders of individuals. Similarly, this was why, before Heidegger,
Dostoevsky's underground man of acute consciousness would be perceived by
society as crazy.[40] The problem is that the philosophical worldview of the
ordinary, everyday person serves as a constriction of the possibilities for both
the individual and society. It was this constriction that needed to be opened up
as far as Heidegger was concerned. Here, Heidegger offered psychology a
way to free itself from its unduly constrictive and exclusionary worldview.

The psychologist, Louis Sass observed close parallels between the
worldviews of many schizophrenics and those of philosophers.[41] Heidegger
and Sass shared as part of their respective views that both philosophers and
some forms of mental disorders have certain major characteristics in common.
For example, both saw the two as often being preoccupied with a heightened
form of conscious awareness that involves either an exclusive and dominant
preoccupation with reason or some other mode of alienation.[42]

What, we might ask, is common to mental disorders and
philosophical reflection? We only have space to list several of the primary
prima facie resemblances. First, both often typically engage in *alternative
ways* of thinking from those of the everyday person and/or the mainstream
viewpoint of one's society at large. A second commonality is a consequence
of the first: both groups tend to experience various forms of alienation from
the group that represents (according to them) "normality." Third, it is
commonly known that both expend enormous energies on abstract ideas, and
seem to be tormented by metaphysically oriented problems. Finally, both
groups tend to be highly introspectively focused.

---

[38] Ludwig Wittgenstein, *Remarks on the Foundations of Mathematics*, trans. G.E.M.
Anscombe (Oxford: Basil Blackwell, 1956), 157.
[39] Wittgenstein, *Philosophical Investigations*, 51.
[40] Fyodor Dostoevsky, *Notes from Underground*, trans. Ralph Matlaw (New York: E.
P. Dutton, 1960), 6.
[41] See Louis Sass, *Madness and Modernism: Insanity in the Light of Modern Art,
Literature, and Thought* (Cambridge: Harvard University Press, 1994), and Louis Sass,
The Paradoxes of Delusion: Wittgenstein, Schreber, and the Schizophrenic Mind
(Ithica: Cornell University Press, 1994).
[42] Sass, *Madness and Modernism*, 10.

To some extent such commonalities are understandable given the fact that such philosophers have delved deeply into the meaning and value of existence itself. The attempt to think deeply can at times—when extreme—manifest itself as a pathological condition. The conclusions of their ruminations may be seen to have easily led them to depression, at the very least. For example, one such conclusion shared by both Heidegger and Nietzsche is that sheer existence itself is a burden with which we must cope if we are to live.[43] This for most people is surely a depressing prospect.

Another way to address this question is to note that it was Nietzsche and Dostoevsky as astute observers of human psychology who independently came to the conclusion that acute consciousness, while identifying the aspects of the universe that matter to us and why, is both a danger and a disease.[44] Couple this insight with the idea that both philosophy and madness typically involve *alternative ways of thinking* (i.e., as opposed to the everyday norm) then it comes as no surprise that the two substantially overlap. It was Heidegger and Freud who offered their own powerful respective ways of coping with these forms of acute consciousness.

In his early philosophy, Heidegger, through his acute modes of awareness, challenged the claims to *exclusivity* made by rationality in appropriately characterizing human existence. The irony is, of course, that this action itself was taken by some to constitute additional evidence that Heidegger was insane. To see why, consider how "madness" has come to be typically defined in the broadest terms by the tradition: "Madness is *ir*rationality, a condition involving *decline* or even disappearance of the role of rational factors in the organization of human conduct and experience."[45] This definition has dominated our tradition extending back to Plato who viewed madness as the rational soul that has succumbed to its "appetites." It continues to characterize contemporary times as well, for example, in Freudian metapsychology, which held precisely the same notion. One of Heidegger's goals was to act precisely as a watershed against the grip with which the rationality of the enlightenment dominated us.

Clearly, it was another goal of Heidegger's acute mode of awareness to disclose the deepest, most primordial significance of human existence. The psychiatrist Karl Jaspers noticed a significant parallel with madness here, that many who are considered to be crazy believe themselves to have done precisely the same thing: that "they have grasped the profoundest meanings; have had "metaphysical experiences."[46] Interestingly, Heidegger was not sympathetic to Jaspers point. In a review of Jasper's *Psychology of*

---

[43] Friedrich Nietzsche, *Werke in drei Banden*, vol. 3, ed. Karl Schlechta (Munchen: Hanser, 1965), 754.

[44] Dostoevsky, *Notes from the Underground*, 6.

[45] Sass, *Madness and Modernism*, 1, authors' emphasis.

[46] Karl Jaspers, *General Psychopathology* (Baltimore: Johns Hopkins University Press, 1997), 114-15.

Worldviews, Heidegger simply dismissed this perspective "as philosophy as *self-affliction.*"[47]

However, the contemporary clinical psychologist, Louis Sass reported a variety of ways in which patients with severe mental illnesses mirror some primary concerns of Heidegger's early philosophy. For example, some are "obsessed" with the fact that there *are* any objects at all (i.e., Why is there something rather than nothing?).[48] Some are preoccupied with *the mere being of a particular object* (i.e., their attention becomes "fixated").[49] Finally, Heidegger had indicated the problem of using everyday words to construct ontological descriptions. Words typically work best in describing discrete objects, but are ill equipped to describe ontological aspects that involved the indissolubly interconnected unity of what we call "world" *as we live it.* When a person strives to do so, she or he will seem "mad" to those who have no understanding of or are not sympathetic to what the person is trying to convey.[50] Sass pointed out that mental patients have occasionally experienced precisely the same problem.[51]

One parallel that Sass overlooked was that Heidegger, like some schizophrenics, saw himself as a "conduit" of sorts for the manifestation of some other being. For example, Heidegger said: "It thinks in me. I cannot resist it."[52] It was *a thinking by Being* through him.

In some cases, the above commonalities tend to revolve around the question concerning the meaning of life. "What is the meaning of life?" This is a question that many of us raise at one time or another during our lifetimes. However, perhaps what distinguishes philosophers and those with mental disorders from the "normal" population is the extent of the focus on this issue, especially when such ponderings exclude other concerns. On one level Heidegger and Freud answered this question in precisely the same way: there is no global or overarching meaning to human existence—no *deep* meaning. This recognition, at least initially, involves the breakdown of significance in the human condition. However, each reacted to this breakdown in very

---

[47] Safranski, *Martin Heidegger*, 119.
[48] Sass, *Madness and Modernism*, 49.
[49] Ibid., 33.
[50] This is point is illustrated for example, in Ingeborg Bachmann, *Die Kritische Aufnahme der Existentialphilosophie Martin Heidegger*, ed. Rober Pichl (Munich: Piper, 1985); Rickert, *Die Logik des Pradikats und das Problem der Ontologie*, (Heidelberg, 1930); Hermann Philipse, *Heidegger's Philosophy of Being*, (Princeton: Princeton University Press, 1998); and Edward Witherspoon, "Logic and the Inexpressible in Frege and Heidegger," in *Journal of the History of Philosophy*, 40:1, (2002). Most famously, Rudolph Carnap derisively mocked Heidegger's idea that "the nothing nothings" as a flagrant "violation of logical syntax." Rudolph Carnap, "The Elimination of Metaphysics Through Logical Analysis of Language" (1932), in *Logical Positivism*, ed. by A. J. Ayer (New York: The Free Press, 1959).
[51] Sass, *Madness and Modernism*, 190.
[52] Safranski, *Martin Heidegger*, 315.

different ways. For Heidegger *it is an opportunity* to take hold of one's possibilities and create one's existence. For Freud, *it is a sickness* to be treated. The client must reengage his or her emotions, free up the energies that have been blocked and become emotionally engaged once again in everyday life.

In the context of our play, the engagement of both Heidegger's and Freud's perspectives is graphically illustrated. For example, from Heidegger's point of view, when the client in therapy is experiencing genuine Angst, it is typical for professionals across the psychological community (e.g., therapists, psychiatrists, analysts, etc.) not only to fail to recognize this experience for what it is, but misidentify it as a form of anxiety that is ultimately reducible to some kind of fear. They then attempt to eliminate the fear through a number of methods. Having done so, they have endeavored to "cure" an intrinsic aspect of the human condition using methods that exacerbate the situation. It is this danger that Heidegger warned against at all costs.

The basis of Heidegger's psychological issues, however, was predominately an alienation from his emotions, instincts, and the body. For Heidegger, Freudian theory was just another form of "irrationalism:" "Irrationalism, as the counterplay of rationalism, talks about things to which rationalism is blind, it does so only with a squint."[53] It does so with a squint because it is exclusively ontically involved, and oblivious to the ontological dimension of human existence. The problem is that this served as a rationale for Heidegger to ignore the role of his instinctual energies and certain emotions within his own historical existence. The irony is that the experience of Angst (though misunderstood by such a scientistic perspective), which has as its positive outcome the expansion of a person's possibilities—as that being which bestows meaning within its field of existence—can *act as a constrictor* of an individual's existence by becoming the dominant mode of attunement (or at least perceived as such) and thereby disengaging one from any other possible modes of attunement (i.e., emotions such as fear, guilt, etc.). That is, Angst could be used to cover-up one's fear or guilt precisely so that one does not have to face up to it authentically. In the context of our play, this is precisely what happened to Heidegger. Here psychoanalysis offers Heidegger a means by which he can authentically face his unresolved emotions.

Freud's point would be that by providing such an alternative (such as phenomenological intuition), this ontological mode of comportment might squeeze out the importance of the emotions, resulting in a kind of emotional disengagement with the world and thereby a breakdown of sorts. From Freud's perspective, occasionally patients use the resources of their intellects to avoid recognition of hidden motives that led their intellects to develop those resources in the first place. In the context of our play, one might argue that Heidegger did just this. By being preoccupied with the "ontological" considerations of the situation (e.g., that we have no foundation for our being),

---

[53] Heidegger, *Being and Time*, 173.

Heidegger may not have allowed one of his "slumbering possibilities" to come to the fore. In this case, one such possibility was Heidegger's hidden guilt concerning his affair with Hannah Arendt. From a Freudian perspective, this affair represents Heidegger's "cauldron of seething desires," uniting and tearing apart simultaneously. For given the historical context, this was no quotidian affair. Arendt was of Jewish heritage and Heidegger remained a member of the Nazi party for decades. Given Heidegger's philosophical and political views it was problematic for him to genuinely love the person and yet despise the very fabric of her genetic heritage. Or in Freudian terms, how could Heidegger reconcile his instinctual drives to unite ("Eros") *and* tear asunder ("Thanatos")? And on another, yet interrelated, level, how was it possible for Heidegger to embrace his own authenticity on this matter while not falling prey to the destructive forces of the Nazi "they-self" mentality? It is important to observe here that the above historical context coupled with Heidegger's need to conceal the affair from the church, his family, and the public domain resulted in what Freud would call an "overdetermination" of Heidegger's motives.[54] It is possible that Heidegger's mental collapse was the result of these blatantly contradictory modes of being-in-the-world. We speculate that in order to shield himself from his unconscious guilt, existential anxiety (Angst) ironically served to conceal his hidden motivation. The intellect, then, assumed the superior position by which the ontical emotional levels were simply ignored. Hence, it *could* very well be and sometimes is the case that psychologists are conflating Angst with fear (or some kind of psychological anxiety). However, in this case, it is ironic that Heidegger's brilliance and specific conceptual apparatus was employed to protect him from an authentic recognition of himself. It is here that psychology could save him from himself and offer some much needed assistance.

One major concern of this book is the role of the *breakdown* of significance in the human condition. It is about our no longer being comfortable in our world as this manifests itself in our capacity and incapacity to face who we *are*. It is also about how we go about *coping* with this breakdown of significance. For Heidegger, it is about authentically, resolutely creating the meaning of our lives while at the same time recognizing that there is no foundation to our existence. For Freud it is about uncovering our hidden motivations so that our energies are freed-up to pursue a less encumbered life of meaning and richer significance. These two approaches are mutually reinforcing and beneficial.

---

[54] "Overdetermination for Freud meant that act x had it's source as a multiplicity of different, yet interrelated motives.

Bibliography

Arendt, H. and M. Heidegger. *Letters 1925-1975*. Edited by Ursula Ludz, translated by Andrew Shields. New York: Harcourt, 2004.

Askay, R. "A Philosophical Dialogue Between Heidegger and Freud." In *Journal of Philosophical Research*. Vol. XXIV, 1999, 415-43.

Askay, R. and J. Farquhar. *Apprehending the Inaccessible: Freudian Psychoanalysis and Existential Phenomenology*. Evanston: Northwestern University Press, 2006.

Beimel, Walter and Hans Saner, eds. *Martin Heidegger/Karl Jaspers Briefwechsel 1920-1963*. Frankfurt am Main; Klostermann; Munich: Piper, 1990.

Binswanger, L. *Sigmund Freud: Reminiscences of a Friendship*. Translated by Norbert Guterman. New York and London, 1957.

————. "The Existential Analysis School of Thought." Translated by Ernest Angel, in *Existence: A New Dimension in Psychiatry and Psychology*, edited by Rollo May, Ernest Angel, and Henri Ellenberger. New York: Simon and Schuster, 1958. 191-213.

————. "Insanity as Life-Historical Phenomenon and as Mental Disease: The Case of Ilse." Translated by Ernest Angel, in *Existence: A New Dimension in Psychiatry and Psychology*, edited by Rollo May, Ernest Angel, and Henri Ellenberger. New York: Simon and Schuster, 1958, 214-36.

————. "The Case of Ellen West." Translated by Werner Mendel and Joseph Lyons, in *Existence: A New Dimension in Psychiatry and Psychology*, edited by Rollo May, Ernest Angel, and Henri Ellenberger. New York: Simon and Schuster, 1958, 237-364.

————. "Dank an Husserl." In *Edmund Husserl, 1859-1959*. Edited by Van Breda. The Hauge: Nijhoff, 1959.

————. *Being-in-the-World: Selected Papers of Ludwig Binswanger*. Translated by Jacob Needleman. New York: Harper and Row, 1963.

————. *Grundformen und Erkenntnis menschlichen Daseins ("Basic Forms and Cognition of Human Dasein")*. Zurich: Niehans, 1964.

————. *Ausgewahlte Werke Band 3*. Edited by M. Herzog. Heidelberg: Asanger Verlag, 1994.

Boehlich, W., ed. *The Letters of Sigmund Freud to Eduard Silberstein.* Translated by Arnold Pomerans. Cambridge: Belknap Press, 1990.

Boss, M. *Analysis of Dreams.* Translated by Arnold Pomerans. London: Rider, 1957.

———. *Existential Foundations of Medicine and Psychology.* Translated by Steven Conway and Anne Cleaves. New York: Aronson, 1979.

———. *Psychoanalysis and Daseinsanalysis.* Translated by Ludwig Lefebre. New York: Dacapo Press, 1982.

Dostoevsky, F. *Notes from Underground.* Translated by Ralph Matlaw. New York: E. P. Dutton, 1960.

Ettinger, E. *Hannah Arendt/Martin Heidegger.* New Haven: Yale University Press, 1995.

Farias, Victor. *Heidegger and Nazism.* Translated by Paul Burrell and Gabriel Ricci. Philadelphia: Temple University Press, 1989.

Freud, S. *The Origins of Psychoanalysis: Letters to Willheilm Fliess.* Translated by Eric Mosbacher and J. Strachey. New York: Basic Books, 1954.

———. *The Standard Edition of the Complete Psychological Works of Sigmund Freud.* Translated and edited by James Strachey. London: Hogarth Press, 1960.

———. *The Letters of Sigmund Freud.* Edited by Ernst Freud and translated by Tania Stern and James Stern. New York: Basic Books, 1975.

Freud, S. and Carl Jung. *Freud/Jung Correspondence.* Vol. 1. Princeton: Princeton University Press, 1974.

Frie, R. *Subjectivity and Intersubjectivity in Modern Philosophy and Psychoanalysis: A Study of Sartre, Binswanger, Lacan, and Habermas.* New York: Rowman and Littlefield, 1997.

Gregory, Richard, ed. *The Oxford Companion to The Mind.* Oxford: Oxford University Press, 1987.

Heidegger, M. *Being and Time.* Translated by John Macquarrie and E. Robinson. New York: Harper and Row, 1962.

———. *Discourse On Thinking.* Translated by John M. Anderson and E. Hans Freund. Evanston: Harper and Row, 1966.

———. *Basic Writings.* Edited by David Krell. New York: Harper and Row, 1977.

———. *The Basic Problems of Phenomenology.* Translated by Albert Hofstadter. Bloomington: Indiana University Press, 1982.

———. *The Metaphysical Foundations of Logic.* Translated by Michael Heim. Bloomington: Indiana University Press, 1984.

———. *History of the Concept of Time: Prolegomena.* Translated by Theodore Kisiel. Bloomington: Indiana University Press, 1985.

———. *Nietzsche.* Vols. 1-4. Translated by David Krell. San Francisco: Harper, 1991.

———. *Parmenides.* Translated by André Schuwer and Richard Rojcewicz. Bloomington: Indiana University Press, 1992.

———. *The Fundamental Concepts of Metaphysics: World, Finitude, Solitude.* Translated by William McNeill and Nicholas Walker. Bloomington: Indiana University Press, 1995.

———. *Pathmarks.* Translated by W. McNeil. Cambridge: Cambridge University Press, 1998.

———. *Contributions to Philosophy (From Enowning).* Translated by Parvis Emad and Kenneth Maly. Bloomington: Indiana University Press, 1999.

———. *Zollikon Seminars: Protocols—Conversations—Letters.* Edited by Medard Boss, and translated by Franz Mayr and Richard Askay. Evanston: Northwestern University Press, 2001.

Hoeller, K., ed. *Heidegger and Psychology.* Seattle: Review of Existential Psychology and Psychiatry, 1988.

Jaspers, Karl. *General Psychopathology.* Baltimore: Johns Hopkins University Press, 1997.

Jones, E. *The Life and Works of Sigmund Freud.* New York: Basic Books, 1955.

Lao Tsu. *Tao Te Ching.* Translated by Gia-Fu Feng and Jane English. New York: Vintage Books, 1989.

Lukács, G. *Marxism and Human Liberation.* London: New Left Books, 1971.

May, Rollo, Ernest Angel, and Henri Ellenberger, eds. *Existence: A New Dimension in Psychiatry and Psychology.* New York: Simon and Schuster, 1958.

Nietzsche, Friedrich. *Werke in drei Banden.* Vol. 3. Edited by K Schlechta. Munchen: Hanser, 1965.

————. *The Will to Power.* Translated by Walter Kaufmann and R.J. Hollingdale. New York: Vintage Books, 1968.

————. *The Portable Nietzsche.* Translated and edited by Walter Kaufmann. New York: Viking Press, 1970.

————. *Beyond Good and Evil: Prelude to a Philosophy of the Future.* Translated by Walter Kaufmann. New York: Vintage Books, 1989.

Nunberg, H. and E. Federn, eds. *Minutes of the Vienna Psychoanalytic Society.* Translated by M. Nunberg. New York: International Universities Press, 1975.

Ott, H. *Martin Heidegger: A Political Life.* Translated by A. Blunden. London: Basic Books, 1993.

Petzet, H. *Encounters and Dialogues with Martin Heidegger 1929-1976.* Translated by Parvis Emad and Kenneth Maly. Chicago: University of Chicago Press, 1993.

Safranski, R. *Martin Heidegger: Between Good and Evil.* Translated by Ewald Osers. Cambridge: Harvard University Press, 1998.

————. *Nietzsche: A Philosophical Biography.* Translated by Shelley Frisch. New York: Norton, 2002.

Sass, Louis. *Madness and Modernism: Insanity in the Light of Modern Art, Literature, and Thought.* Cambridge: Harvard University Press, 1994.

————. *The Paradoxes of Delusion: Wittgenstein, Schreber, and the Schizophrenic Mind.* Ithica: Cornell University Press, 1994.

Scharfstein, Ben-Ami. *The Philosophers: Their Lives and the Nature of Their Thought.* Oxford: Oxford University Press, 1980.

Scheler, M. *Reality and Resistance.* Evanston: Northwestern University Press, 1927.

Spiegelberg, H. *Phenomenology in Psychology and Psychiatry: A Historical Introduction.* Evanston: Northwestern University Press, 1972.

Vaidyanathan, T.G. and Jeffrey J. Kripal, eds. *Vishnu on Freud's Desk: A Reader in Psychoanalysis and Hinduism.* Delhi: Oxford University Press, 1999.

Wittgenstein, L. *Remarks on the Foundations of Mathematics.* Translated by G.E.M. Anscombe. Oxford: Basil Blackwell, 1956.

————. *Philosophical Investigations.* Translated by G. E. M. Anscombe. New York: Macmillan Company, 1971.